Two Ways About It

TWO WAYS ABOUT IT

THE INSIDE AND OUTSIDE OF PLAYWRITING

JOHN LAZARUS

J. GORDON SHILLINGFORD
PUBLISHING INC

Two Ways About It: The Inside and Outside of Playwriting
© 2023 John Lazarus

Editor: Glenda MacFarlane
Cover design by Doowah Design
Photo of John Lazarus by Lin Bennett
Printed and bound in Canada on 100% post-consumer recycled paper.

Excerpts from the following works appear by permission of the authors and/or publishers: Page 19, page 65, page 184, page 185, page 195, page 206: Richard Greenblatt, *Text and Context: The Operative Word* (Winnipeg: J. Gordon Shillingford Publishing Inc, 2021), p. 180, p. 48, pp. 170, 173, pp. 172-176, p. 88, p. 143, 144. Page 30: Betty Edwards, *Drawing on the Right Side of the Brain* (Los Angeles: Jeremy P. Tarcher, Inc., 1989), p. 38. Pages 43–44: Kathleen Oliver, *Swollen Tongues*, 1999. Pages 66–67: Alan Ayckbourn, Part 2, pp. 66–67: *The Crafty Art of Playmaking* (London: Faber and Faber, 2002), pp. 12-14. Used by permission of Faber and Faber. Pages 119–120: Marie Humber Clements, *Tombs of the Vanishing Indian*, from *Refractions: Solo*, ed. Donna-Michelle St. Bernard and Yvette Nolan (Toronto: Playwrights Canada Press, 2014), p. 4. Pages 120–121: Erin Shields, *Soliciting Temptation* (Toronto: Playwrights Canada Press, 2015), pp. 5–6. Page 137: Jenn Stephenson, *Insecurity: Perils and Products of Theatres of the Real* (Toronto: University of Toronto Press, 2019), p. 11. Page 149: Annie Baker, *The Flick* (New York: Theatre Communications Group, 2014). pp. 4–5. Used by permission of Theatre Communications Group. Page 162: Colleen Murphy, *The Society for the Destitute Presents Titus Bouffonius* (Winnipeg: Scirocco Drama, 2021). Pages 168–169: David Mamet, "A Playwright in Hollywood," *Writing in Restaurants* (New York: Penguin Books, 1986), p. 76. Used by permission of Penguin Books.

Library and Archives Canada Cataloguing in Publication

Title: Two ways about it : the inside and outside of playwriting / John Lazarus.
Names: Lazarus, John, 1947– author.
Description: Includes index.
Identifiers: Canadiana 2023051958X | ISBN 9781990738296 (softcover)
Subjects: LCSH: Playwriting. | LCSH: Drama—Technique.
Classification: LCC PN1661 .L39 2023 | DDC 808.2—dc23

We acknowledge the financial support of the Canada Council for the Arts, the Government of Canada, the Manitoba Arts Council, and the Government of Manitoba for our publishing program.

J. Gordon Shillingford Publishing
P.O. Box 86, RPO Corydon Avenue, Winnipeg, MB Canada R3M 3S3
www.jgshillingford.com

*This book is dedicated to
Aidan, Arabella, and Elizabeth,
whether they ever use it or not*

TABLE OF CONTENTS

The argument that started all this. Where it went from there. About this book

PART 1
GETTING STARTED

Why don't stories happen by themselves? The M word. Digression: the audience knows more than the characters. Keep working both ends of the notebook. Another form of the duality: the exciting and the believable. The two sides of the brain: a debunked but useful theory. A list of examples of the dual nature of the work. Comedy, drama, or non-binary? A word to the Absurdists

The subject: what to write about. Starting with plot or starting with character. The seven sources. A cautionary note about writing real people. Establishing the stakes. On triggers and warnings. Theme versus message, or: what are plays for?

Originality. Two questionable takes on originality. Appropriation: the predicament. Appropriation: a solution. Research

PART 2
THE TWO WAYS: PLOT AND DIALOGUE

Plotting is fun! (though not everyone agrees). Chat plays. The Guide Sentence. The plot begins: interrupting a routine. On climaxes and dénouements. Building a plot with Cause-and-Effect. Cause-and-Effect in Relatively Speaking. Cause-and-Effect in Hamlet. Cause-and-Effect in Dreaming and Duelling. Cause-and-Effect: summing up and moving on

PART 3
THE OTHER STUFF YOU DO ALONE

Foreword

Kevin Loring

John Lazarus is one of the reasons I am a playwright today. John has been a mentor, a colleague, a supporter, and a friend for the entirety of my career. His love for the art form is limitless. He is a theatre person's theatre person, and this book will inform and inspire yet another generation of aspiring playwrights to create worlds and characters for actors and designers, directors, and audience members to fall in love with. John teaches the fundamentals of the craft, breaks down the realities of the business, and tells the honest truth about what it takes to be a working playwright, with honesty, humour, and experience.

My playwriting career began in John Lazarus's class at Studio 58, Langara College in Vancouver. It was mandatory for acting students to take his class, so I had no choice in the matter. Lucky for me, it was one of the best things to ever happen to an aspiring theatre student with almost zero experience on stage. Up until my being accepted into "Studio," as alumni call it, I had only been in two plays in my whole life. And although I created some epic role-playing campaigns in my youth, I had never written a play before. So as the least likely of theatre students, everything was new to me, especially playwriting.

If I were to summarize John's class at Studio 58 I would say that it was about giving ourselves permission. Permission to be bold and adventurous and, most importantly, permission to fail. And for an artist this is the most important lesson to learn. One of the hardest obstacles to overcome as an artist is the fear of failure. The fear of getting it wrong or writing something stupid, or even worse, boring. John's playwriting class was for acting students (and the odd production student) so there was no real expectation or pressure to be good at it, no one was expecting us to go off and become actual playwrights—if we did, great, but really, we were there to gain an understanding of the process of writing a play so that we could take that experience and understanding and put it into our acting toolbox.

The freedom to fail in a school renowned for excellence and rigour was like a release valve for my imagination. It was in this class that I discovered a love for playwriting. John would encourage us to spit up whatever creative mess we were considering, and, with a readily available supply of fresh brilliant young acting talent to rip into the pages every week, we would try out our bad ideas. We'd discuss each piece with vigour and bald honesty, learning to take constructive criticism and to ditch what wasn't helpful, to look at the work with a critical eye but also with the bravery to hold onto our vision. So many of the principles that I live by as a professional playwright today were established in his class: how to receive input from a workshop setting, what is a useful note, the value of bad writing, and when to kill your darlings. The craft of playwriting and how the rigour of craft can be a lifeline when all else seems to fail.

I learned to love the rewriting process. We'd examine what worked and what didn't, the actors would chime in with their responses to the work, and John would always be there too with his infectious giggle and his wise, sage words of encouragement, "Remember, writing is rewriting."

I come to playwriting from the perspective of being an actor, so the idea of being inside the characters as you are writing them and flipping the notebook to look down at them from the perspective of the creator of the worlds they inhabit really resonates and excites me. There can be freedom in structure too, and having a sense of structure as you are writing is something that John always encouraged—even as he encouraged us to let go of that structure to find the flow of action and intention, story and character, speech, and setting.

The authority and freedom of creating worlds is the intoxicant that keeps me dreaming for the stage. Of course, any delusions of power are always tempered by the humility that comes from an understanding and appreciation of the craft, the history, tradition, rigour, resilience, and relentless commitment from the community that is required to bring a show to the stage. And as all writers can attest, it can truly be a lonely profession that may occasionally pay you a few dollars for your many hundreds of hours of labour. But when the lights go down and the actors take their places, there is no greater intoxicant than seeing your vision realized, and your words spoken by a team of artists and technicians working in concert to bring your dreams to reality. This book is like having John in your corner, rooting for you, cheering on your successes, reassuring you when you fail, and reminding you that what you are doing isn't easy—but it's worth it!

June 2023

Kevin Loring is an accomplished Canadian playwright, actor, and director. He is currently the Artistic Director, Indigenous Theatre, at the National Arts Centre

Introduction

How I Became a Playwright, and How This Book Can Protect You from Becoming a Playwright the Way I Did

The argument that started all this

It is a couple of weeks before my 30th birthday, in the early winter of 1977, and I'm sitting in a theatre in Vancouver, having a silent, internal argument with myself which is about to change my life. A play is being performed on the stage in front of me, but I'm not paying much attention to it. I don't have to. I know it all too well. I wrote it. It's called *Midas*, it's a comedy based on ancient myths about the King of Phrygia, and it's a terrible play. So I'm arguing with myself about what, if anything, to do next.

Midas is my first full-length effort. At this point in my young career, I've been calling myself a playwright for about seven years. I started writing short one-act plays in 1970 because I enjoyed writing dialogue and thought I was good at it. A well-meaning friend told me that Harold Pinter created his masterpieces by improvising dialogue, so I set about writing short plays made of improvised dialogue.

Some of the plays I've written this way have worked, and some have not, and by now, in 1977, I still don't know what has made the difference. I have noticed that in the plays that have succeeded, a story has somehow generated itself, and in the plays that have failed, a story has not, but I've been assuming that that's beyond my control.

I have no mentors. In Canada, playwriting, and professional theatre in general, virtually began with my generation. Around 1970, when I graduated from theatre school, the federal government was handing out grants to start small groups of different kinds, many of them theatre companies, which were now suddenly looking for Canadian plays to produce. In spite of some brave, eccentric pioneers who came before us,[1] there haven't been many English-language Canadian scripts lying about, so we've been writing our own.

It's been exciting to be a member of this first widespread generation, but the downside has been the lack of older experts to teach us how. My few glimpses into books on the subject have not proven useful. But Canadian playwriting at this time is still a novelty and a popular cause, so my early attempts have been produced, and critics and audiences have been lenient and encouraging. One of my favourite quotes, from a favourable review of one of my early plays: "Locally-written theatre CAN be good."[2] It's been a process of public on-the-job training, with tolerant responses.

And now, a local theatre company has committed to producing my first full-length effort, on the basis of a partial first draft. Since then, writing *Midas* has been a nightmare. Most plays get somewhat rewritten during rehearsals for the first production— we'll talk about that later—but this is ridiculous: massive changes, made in a tremendous hurry, with no idea of how to control the process.

Writing this mess that's now on the stage in front of me felt rather like sitting in a mud puddle.[3] The mud was the massive amount of verbiage. When I tried to shove one lump of thick mud forward, other rivers of mud flowed backward around me. If I wanted to move a passage to elsewhere in the play, there were bits within that movable mass that I wanted to keep where they were. If I wanted to cut a section entirely, there would be smaller chunks in it that I wanted to save but didn't know how to. (Does any of this seem familiar?)

---

1   A few: John Coulter, Robertson Davies, Mazo de la Roche, John Herbert, Eric Nicol, James Reaney, Gwen Pharis Ringwood, George Ryga, Herman Voaden. The Québecois were way ahead of us, but their works were not yet in translation.

2   Bob Allen, "An hour turns Cold Beer tepid," *Vancouver Province*, July 18, 1973. (Emphasis his.)

3   This is the polite version.

The process has been further complicated by the fact that I have a day job, and haven't been able to get to rehearsals, so the actors have been rewriting the play in my absence. There are firm rules against this practice, but in this case the cast has been desperate, and in fact, their rewrites have usually been depressingly superior to my original text.

On opening night, about a week before this performance at which I'm arguing with myself, the laughs were infrequent, forced and fitful, and the applause half-hearted. The reviews have been harsh and the houses small. On the night of my argument with myself, there are more actors on stage than audience members in the house. So here's the argument:

> ME: That's it. I'm quitting playwriting. I don't know how to do this.

> MYSELF: Seems a shame. I've given seven years to this art form.

> ME: I know. But look at my friends up there, talented actors, struggling to make this crap work. And with all their talent and skill, is this crap working?

> MYSELF: No, this crap is not working.

> ME: So do I know how to write a play?

> MYSELF: No, I do not. *(Brief silence.)* Well, but at least I know now how *not* to write a play. How not to write a play is by doing what I did to create *this* mess. So maybe how *to* write a play is by doing what I *didn't* do.

> ME: So what didn't I do?

> MYSELF: For one thing, I didn't use plot outlines. I've heard of plot outlines, they're supposed to be useful.

> ME: But plot outlines are boring. They're no fun.[4] With dialogue, I can *show* it to people, it's witty and clever and it's

---

4   "Me" was wrong about this. Plot construction can be great fun, as will be demonstrated later. However, as sometimes happens, this incorrect assumption led somewhere useful.

got the characters' names in capitals and the stage directions in parentheses and it looks like a script! It makes women think I'm artistic! Plot outlines just look like homework.

MYSELF: Yeah, but *without* a plot outline, I made *this* mess.

ME: But I got into playwriting because I love writing dialogue. Does this mean I can't write dialogue until I've finished a plot outline? No dessert until I've had my veggies?

MYSELF: *(Pause.)* How about this: I'll start with a plot outline. And when I get bored, I'll take a bit from my plot outline, and then flip the notebook over to the last page, and start writing that bit out, as dialogue, for fun, as a break from plotting. And if none of that dialogue goes into the play, I don't have to feel bad about it, and if some of it does, that's just an added bonus. Okay?

ME: Yeah, okay, sure, whatever. Let's try that.

Where it went from there

The fact that I stumbled upon that evening is that writing fiction is a dual process. To oversimplify it for now, though I promise to re-complicate it in later chapters: one part of the process consists of constructing the plot from a mental perspective that places us "outside" the play, and the other part consists of getting "inside" the characters' minds and hearts and improvising dialogue from their point of view.

My next play after that conversation, *Dreaming and Duelling*, was written this way, was well received, and set me on a path which I am still investigating and developing with great pleasure.[5] Over the years I've kept refining the technique; but "flipping the notebook," as I still call it, continues to form the basis for all my playwriting and teaching. Part of the reason that I teach, and that I'm writing this book, is to try to be the mentor I never had, for other emerging playwrights. My hope is that this book may spare you the years I spent writing haphazardly.

---

5   *Dreaming and Duelling* was also a collaboration with my then-wife, Joa Lazarus, who is credited with co-authorship.

About this book

Part One looks at how to get started, and some basic principles. Part Two explores those "Two Ways About It"—the two sides of the process, plot and dialogue—with a couple of chapters devoted to each side. Part Three guides you through the other aspects of the writing that you do alone. And Part Four guides you through the work you do with other people—workshops, readings, rehearsals, productions, publication—along with a chapter on the business of playwriting in Canada, and an inspirational, wrap-up, feel-good final chapter.

It's structured like this because playwriting is both a solitary and a collaborative art form. Scripts are merely blueprints, ground plans, for the real works of art, which are the productions. It's easy to forget that, because we spend so much time writing the script and so comparatively little time in rehearsal; because scripts endure and productions don't; and because some of our greatest writers have been playwrights, and many scripts also happen to be great literature. But scripts are not intended to be works of art unto themselves, any more than a great painter's preliminary sketches are intended to be works of art, even if some of them are beautiful enough to hang, framed, on museum walls. [6]

This is a book on *play*-writing—rather than screenwriting, novels and other forms—because playwriting is the form I know best, and because for all the popularity of other media, live theatre shows no signs of going away. However, I hope it will also be useful to writers of fiction in other forms and media. Many principles of *any* art form can be applied to *all* art forms. My mother, Selma Lazarus, was a painter, and some of the principles she explained to me about painting are also useful for playwriting.

This book can teach you the *craft* of playwriting, but not the *art*. Art is what happens when you interpret your own emotions, experiences and insights through craft. You already have, and will continue to gain, those emotions, experiences and insights. I'm hoping this book will help you develop the craft with which to

---

6   There is a form called "closet drama," popular in the 18th and 19th centuries: play scripts meant not for performance, but to be read privately. This book will not be dealing with that form.

shape them. You are also entitled to your own tastes, and this book will not try to dictate to you what kinds of plays you should be writing. You can use these techniques to create dark, angry tragedy or sunlit, romantic comedy, or whatever other style appeals to you.

Similarly, the techniques this book describes may seem fairly conventional, and many of the examples given are from conventional work, but again, that's where your own taste and experience come in. This approach doesn't have to result in un-adventurous theatre. You can use it to create the wildest avant-garde onstage art you can imagine.

Among the examples offered in this book, I draw on some of my own work and experiences, including a complete 10-minute play in Chapter 6. These examples are not here due to any illusions I may have about their brilliance, but simply because I have personal knowledge of how they got written.

Please assume that every statement, except for plain facts, begins with the unwritten words, "In my humble opinion," and that every sentence telling you to do something begins with the unwritten words, "You might want to consider trying this out." And please assume that we both know that every rule, guideline, principle or suggestion in this book comes loaded with exceptions.

The Toronto director and actor Richard Greenblatt has written an excellent book on directing: *Text and Context: The Operative Word*. In a chapter on working with playwrights and new plays, Greenblatt writes:

> There is no one right way to write a play. There is no one right way to tell a story, or to reveal character, or narrative, or conflict, or anything else that a play might contain. To say, "This is how plays are written" is limiting and presumptuous in the extreme.[7]

Absolutely right. Of course, I hope you'll try the techniques described in this book and find them helpful, but don't assume that I'm suggesting they're the only correct way to do it. Look for

---

7   Richard Greenblatt, *Text and Context: The Operative Word* (Winnipeg: J. Gordon Shillingford, 2021), 180.

others as well, and if you find an approach contrary to mine that results in a successful play, let me know and I'll try to be there on opening night to cheer you on.

Now, let's explore this ever-changing, endlessly fascinating discipline together.

PART 1

GETTING STARTED

The Two Ways About It

Why don't stories happen by themselves?

Many playwrights do the same thing I did for the seven years it took me to discover my technique. They put a group of characters onstage together, give them something to talk about, wait for a story to generate itself, and get baffled and frustrated when it doesn't. Sometimes the results actually get to the stage, where they bore the audience. Some of these are what I call "chat plays": characters sitting around comfortably, discussing offstage issues.

It's not enough. We want to see characters being challenged, with problems that they are *forced* to solve, so that they must show us what they're made of. An old piece of advice for writers recommends that you put your characters up in a tree, throw rocks at them, and bring them down again. One useful way to lay out this recipe—and I'll be repeating this—is with four words beginning with CH: *Characters*, facing *Challenges*, going through *Changes* and making *Choices*.

But stories—i.e., the Challenges—don't just appear by themselves, and Characters tend not to supply them. On the contrary, they try to avoid them. The reason is so obvious that people don't often mention it, but it's crucial. It is that *characters labour under a delusion: they don't know they're in a play, but think they're experiencing real life.* This means your job is to convey a story to your audience by means of imaginary people who don't *know* that their job is to convey a story to an audience—or that there *is* an audience, or that there's a *you.* In a sense, you must sneak the story across to your audience behind your characters' backs. And this is why your characters won't create an interesting plot for you: because to be in a play with an interesting plot is to be in trouble.[8]

A very common phenomenon in fiction is the reluctant hero. Hamlet doesn't want to kill the King: he puts it off for the entire play. Macbeth doesn't want to kill the King: it takes three witches and his wife to talk him into it. Frodo doesn't want to go drop the ring in the volcano: he'd rather stay home in the Shire, marry a cute barmaid, have a lot of kids and smoke his pipe. This is true of comedy too, because the characters don't know it's supposed to be funny. Those women in drag in Shakespeare's comedies are disguised for safety, not for fun or gender-queer expression; the first hour of *The Winter's Tale* has all the makings of a tragedy; Malvolio in *Twelfth Night* is put through Hell; and Hermia at the beginning of *A Midsummer-Night's Dream* faces a predicament as dire as Juliet's.

So your characters—being, let's hope, smart enough to be interesting—will look for ways to weasel out of the challenges you set for them. They want to solve their problems early, go home, and be safe, comfy, and boring to watch. This leaves you with the job of finding more reasons to keep them in interesting difficulties. Having to invent the plot yourself is the price your characters demand of you for putting them through entertaining, sometimes brutal, experiences.

So your purposes and your characters' purposes are usually opposed to each other. And therefore, *everything in a work of fiction should happen for two reasons: the storyteller's reason and the character's reason.* The storyteller's reason is usually to move the story along, increase the conflict, raise the stakes, introduce the plot complications—all those juicy things that make for an

---

8   Of course, we're talking here about the characters, not the actors. Actors always want to be in plays, with or without interesting plots.

exciting play. And the character's reason is to do whatever will return things to a state of peace and quiet: to give rest to a dead father's ghost, to satisfy an ambitious spouse, or to destroy the Ring and its addictive evil.

The M word

I don't care how high you can kick. I care about why you're kicking.

—Choreographer Judith Marcuse to the dancers, during rehearsals for the dance/drama piece *ICE: beyond cool*, Vancouver, 1997

This brings us to the famous word **motivation**,[9] which means a character's reason that covers up and disguises the storyteller's reason. I use the word "storyteller's," not "playwright's," because this principle also applies to actors, directors, set, costume, sound and lighting designers, composers, choreographers—everyone who deals with the fictional aspects.

The species of storyteller known as an actor is familiar with motivation. Let's say Actor 1 is in rehearsal. In half a page from now, Actor 2 will come in the door and punch Actor 1, leading to the big fight scene. But the door is downstage left, and Actor 1 is upstage right, which is where he had to be for the previous sequence. So the actors and director—knowing it's a play, and knowing what's going to happen because they've read the script— figure out how to "motivate" Actor 1's character to get down left so that he'll be conveniently beside the door when Actor 2 enters: to find a reason for the *character* to move, that will disguise the fact that the *actor* is positioning himself, because the *character* sure isn't going to cross to the door in order to get punched. So Actor 1 proposes, "What if I leave my beer on the table at the beginning of the scene, so that now I can cross down left to get my beer?" And that's his motivation.

A famous passage where it's the playwright who's established the motivation involves Polonius, the King's adviser, hiding behind an

---

9   New terms that you might be unfamiliar with will appear in boldface in this book and be accompanied by definitions.

arras (a free-hanging tapestry) in Queen Gertrude's bedroom, in *Hamlet*, Act 3, Scene 4.

(Before we continue, two digressions. First of all, if you don't know *Hamlet*, just read along: there's enough info here to get you through. But then watch a good movie of it, or see it onstage, because this sequence gets referred to again in this book. Also it's good.

(Secondly, Shakespeare's name will crop up again. It's one of the world's most famous names, and there's a sort of aura of sacredness around it, but he was a fellow struggling playwright, sharing our difficulties, challenges and frustrations. He wasn't perfect: there are plenty of flaws and mistakes in his work. He was merely the best we have—at least in some people's opinions, including mine, though even that honour is currently being called into question. So from now on, I'll refer to him as our fellow playwright, "William.")

William needs Polonius behind that arras so that Hamlet, thinking he's the villain Claudius, can run his sword through the arras, killing the wrong man and setting in motion the rest of the play. But what's Polonius' reason to be there? He doesn't say to Gertrude, "Good Madam, I'll sconce me behind yon arras, that your son Hamlet may kill me." Instead, William gives Polonius his own reasons to be there—first by making him a nosy busybody, and then by making him think it's his own fault that the heir to the throne of Denmark has gone mad, because he's been rejected by Polonius' daughter, on Polonius' orders: motivation.[10]

William does slip up in at least one other play (I told you he's not perfect). He under-motivates Iago, the villain in *Othello*, who decides to destroy Othello for no clear reason. Iago tells us only that—

> I hate the Moor:
> And it is thought abroad, that 'twixt my sheets
> He has done my office. I know not if't be true;
> But I, for mere suspicion in that kind,
> Will do as if for surety.[11]

---

10   Take note, here, the first time that some plot is being described: plot descriptions are customarily in the present tense, as are stage directions. *Plays are always happening now.*

11   Act 1, Sc. 3.

He means that it's rumoured that Othello has slept with Iago's wife Emilia, and whether that's really happened or not, Iago's decided to act as if it is, just in case. But nothing else in the play indicates anything improper between Othello and Emilia—or even that such a rumour exists—so Iago is often cited as an example of an under-motivated villain. (Of course, there may well be a racist component in Iago's hatred: the Elizabethan audience might have understood Iago's resentment at seeing a Black man rise in rank above him, without William's having to explain it.)

If a passage in a play isn't working, it's often because one of those two reasons has been overlooked. Either the storyteller's reason has been forgotten and the story has ground to a halt, or—as with Iago, above—the characters' reasons have been neglected and they're doing what the storyteller wants without their own motivations. One of the commonest examples of unmotivated action is expository dialogue, whose purpose is to give the audience some information, but without enough reasons for the characters to speak it. We'll talk more about **expository** dialogue in Chapter 7.

Digression: the audience knows more than the characters

The characters' delusion that they are actually experiencing real life gives the audience a feeling of superiority, because it's one of several ways that they know more than the characters do. The earliest theatre (e.g., in ancient Athens, in Western drama) retold the society's myths: stories that most adult audience members already knew. The mystery plays of medieval Europe also told familiar stories: theirs were from the Bible.

Elizabethan theatre offered three categories of plays: histories, where many audience members knew the story, and comedies and tragedies, where they knew one crucial fact: whether it would end with the central character dying or getting married. If they knew it was a tragedy and he was going to die, they could pity his attempts to save himself, knowing he didn't have a hope. If they knew it was a comedy and he was going to get married and live happily ever after, they could laugh at his fear of disaster.

Today, when we may not know whether a fictional work will end happily or horribly for the characters, we still know one thing they don't: that it's governed by the rules of fiction, where events tend to link up, rather than the "rules" of our world, which amount to dumb, random coincidence.[12] So the audience's antennae are out, seeking conflict and drama, in a way that the characters' antennae are not, as they seek peace and comfort.

Here's an example from the opening scene of Alan Ayckbourn's 1965 comedy *Relatively Speaking*. A young man, Greg, has just spent the night at the apartment of his girlfriend, Ginny. While she's out of the room, the phone rings. (It's 1965, so there's just one phone, plugged into the wall.) He answers it. Whoever phoned hangs up. He assumes it's a wrong number. End of moment.

If that moment happened in real life, it would indeed be the kind of random event called a wrong number, common in the days of rotary phones, and neither Greg nor Ginny would hear from that person again. But as it's a play, the audience's antennae are out: they assume the caller will be back. (In fact, in this play, the caller phones back immediately, and hangs up again; and that, combined with a few other oddities, begins to arouse Greg's antennae too.)

If that caller did *not* show up again, then after the performance, viewers would say to each other, "What was the deal with the phone call at the beginning? How come nothing came of that?" It would be considered a playwriting flaw, because it's understood that the events in a work of fiction ought to link up with each other and make some kind of sense in a way that the events in real life do not.[13] So the audience interprets events in a way that the characters, in their delusion, cannot—which makes the audience feel smart and superior, which is one of the pleasures of theatre.

---

12 Or so it seems. No offence to theists. This book is not prepared to discuss the existence of God.

13 There are exceptions to this, in the postmodern novel, Theatre of the Absurd, the New Playwriting, etc.: See the section "A Word to the Absurdists" at the end of this chapter.

Keep working both ends of the notebook

You can start with character(s) or with plot (or, less commonly, with setting or theme). If it's characters or plot, then whichever you're more comfortable with, you owe it to yourself to develop the skills for working the other side of the process as well. My students are required to submit, every week, at least some dialogue and at least some notes, which usually include plot outline material. It's a way of emphasizing that both sides of the process—both "ways about it"—are essential.

There will be more about starting by constructing plot, or starting by improvising character, in the next chapter. However, this pair of tasks is just one of several different examples of the double nature of the work. Here are a couple of others.

Another form of the duality: the exciting and the believable

One other way of expressing this duality is to say that a play should be both *exciting* and *believable*. This can be shown as a simple Venn diagram, where each circle represents one of these two qualities, and your play occupies the overlap.

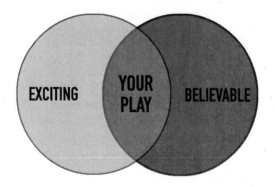

Each of those four CHs we've mentioned—the Characters, the Challenges they face, the Changes they go through and the Choices they make—should ideally be both exciting and believable. Those aren't just two synonyms for "good": they are specific. If a story is believable but not exciting, then it may be one of those chat plays. If it's exciting but not believable, then it may be set in a world of superheroes and supervillains without enough convincing personal reasons to do the things they do, or without skills and limitations that the ordinary mortals in the audience can understand or identify with. A good work of fiction includes both the exciting and the believable.

The *exciting* aspect is usually embedded in the *plot* that you create for your Characters to struggle with, i.e., the Challenges they face. The *believable* aspect usually comes out in the way they deal with it—the Changes they go through and the Choices they make—which is customarily expressed in their dialogue.

A clarification: "believable" does not mean the same as "realistic." Believability is a quality, and realism is a style. Fiction can be realistic but unbelievable: set in our familiar world but written with unconvincing characters. Or fiction can be unrealistic but believable, as with many fantasies—*Lord of the Rings, Harry Potter, Game of Thrones, Narnia, Alice in Wonderland, A Midsummer-Night's Dream*—where the characters seem recognizable, even if they are elves, fairies, trolls, hobbits or talking trees. It also describes musicals: it's not realistic for people to burst into song to express their feelings, but if those feelings are believable, we accept the convention.

The two sides of the brain: a debunked but useful theory

Another way to express this duality is with a 20th-century theory about the human brain: that the two halves of the cerebral cortex have different functions and "personalities." The left brain is described as orderly, methodical, mathematical and organizational, and the right brain is supposed to be spontaneous and playful and improvisational. The American art teacher Betty Edwards wrote a beautiful how-to-draw book called *Drawing on the Right Side of the Brain* (1979), in which she describes the two sides: "The L is foursquare, upright, sensible, direct, true, hard-edged, unfanciful, forceful. The R is curvy, flexible, more playful in its unexpected twists and turns, more complex, diagonal, fanciful."[14]

Recent psychological research has called this theory into question, but the image remains popular, and is a useful tool when we talk about playwriting. If there's any truth to it, then it suggests that the left brain logically constructs the plot, and the playful, intuitive right brain, pretending to be the various characters, improvises the dialogue.

Many cartoons and drawings of the two halves of the brain at work make the right brain look sexy and colourful and a lot more fun than the boring, workaholic left brain. Typically, they show the right brain full of people writing sonnets, painting pictures, playing guitars and making love in fields of flowers, while the left brain is just so many grey workers sitting in grey cubicles. But you need both. Those flowers need frames to grow in, so to speak. And, again, the plot work done on the left side of the brain can be as enjoyable as the right-brain improvisations.

A list of examples of the dual nature of the work

Here's a summation of different ways to think about the two sides of the playwriting process:

On the One Hand:	On the Other Hand:
Plot	Dialogue
Excitement	Believability
Challenges	Changes and Choices
Storyteller's Reasons	Character's Reasons
Action and Exposition	Motivation
Left Brain	Right Brain

---

14 Betty Edwards, *Drawing on the Right Side of the Brain* (Los Angeles: Jeremy P. Tarcher, Inc., 1989), 38.

Comedy, drama, or non-binary?

You may be puzzling over whether to make your play a comedy, a drama, or a blend of both. As indicated earlier, comedy and tragedy used to be clearly delineated. The modern business of mashing them up seems to have begun towards the end of the 19th century, with playwrights like Shaw, Wilde, and Chekhov (who has puzzled generations of students by labeling his plays "comedies").

If your play contains both humour and serious material, you may not want to decide in advance whether to label it a comedy or a drama. You might simply write "A play by…" beneath the title. But if you want to call it a comedy, consider this checklist: are you naturally a witty, humorous sort of person? Do people say you're funny? Do you have a habit of writing humorously? Is your play thickly seeded with funny moments? (You know that expression, "a laugh a minute"? That isn't enough.) And does the play have a happy ending? (Granted, some comedies, "dark comedies," do not.) Otherwise, you may prefer to wait for the audience to tell you whether it's a comedy, a drama, neither, or both.

A word to the Absurdists

As mentioned earlier, this book may appear to teach conventional playwriting. So here's a clarification for the avant-garde / surrealist / Theatre-of-the-Absurd fans.

In 1896 Paris, a writer named Alfred Jarry invented this kind of theatre, with an obscene parody of William's *Macbeth* called *Ubu Roi (King Ubu)* that began a tradition of cutting-edge, avant-garde, irrational theatre which has gone through several mutations and labels, including Surrealism, Theatre of the Absurd, The New Playwriting and In-Yer-Face Theatre. Nowadays it overlaps with Performance Art.

Currently there is also a lively interest in **Post-Dramatic Theatre**, an attempt to engage audiences *without* the kinds of plotted dramatic events that this book teaches. I do get that this is, like minimalist art, an inevitable development. The part I balk at slightly is the prefix "Post-," which implies that un-dramatic theatre is a new development, and that dramatic theatre was an immature phase which it is now time to outgrow—an assumption with which, with all due respect, I disagree.

In any case, I do admire those who can do the kind of work that began with Jarry, and I enjoy a lot of it very much, even though it's not my own forte as a playwright. However, I maintain that however dreamlike and surreal the theatre that you create, it will almost certainly be helped by an active plot or plots. Theatre, music, dance, film and other forms of performance take place through time, as opposed to painting, sculpture, architecture, etc., whose viewers supply the time spent looking at it. Theatre leads the audience through the story, and I believe that the ideal is to keep them wanting to know what happens next.

So even if your ambition is to write the next Absurdist or Post-Dramatic masterpiece(s), I hope you'll find useful stuff in here—if only because the better you understand the rules, the more creatively you can bend or break them. And with that, Absurdists, I respectfully invite you to read on.

2

Starting to Start

Subject, Sources, Stakes, and What Are Plays For?

If you already know what to write about this time, good for you; this chapter might help you with future plays. Various elements are listed in the chapter: the subject matter, where to look for source material, how to set the stakes, and a look at the purpose of plays in terms of message and theme. But you're under no obligation to set your play up with this order of operations. You might find something in the list of source material first, and then develop it into more clearly defined subject matter. You may think about questions of message versus theme before you do anything else. And the matter of stakes tends to recur frequently during the process. It's up to you. This order, however, makes sense to many students.

The subject: what to write about

Write the story you need to tell.

—Judith Thompson to her students,
quoted by Bilal Baig[15]

15 Soraya Roberts, "The Uncertain Stardom of Bilal Baig," *Maclean's Magazine*, Nov. 2, 2022.

In addition to this excellent advice, another way to decide what to write about is to think about events you would not want to take place in your own life. Here's the Ancient Greek philosopher Aristotle, said by some to be the first theatre critic:

> There are some things that upset us if we see them in reality, but that give us pleasure when we see very accurate representations of them: for example, frightening animals, or dead bodies.
>
> —Aristotle, *The Poetics*, circa 330 B.C.E.,
> Chapter 4

Another way to think about a topic is to explore a theme you feel passionate about. Look at your own strongest emotions. Good starting-points include anger, fear, longing—or sympathy with others who are angry, fearful or longing.

Starting with plot or starting with character

We've already mentioned that there are two widely used ways to begin a play. You can begin with a plot and invent characters who will make that plot work, either by being the type who will move things along, or the type who will hate what's happening to them, or both. Or you can begin with a character or characters and invent a plot that will challenge them or bring out their most interesting traits. As also mentioned previously, playwrights sometimes begin their plays with an idea for a setting or theme, but plot and character seem to be the most popular and effective ways of getting started. All these approaches can give rise to excellent work.

The following examples of the two most popular approaches both come from former students at Studio 58, a Vancouver theatre conservatory program where I taught for some years. The example of starting with an idea for a plot, and then coming up with a character who will make that plot work, comes from the first solo show created by Tracey Erin Smith, who went on to found and run a successful theatre and school in Toronto called SOULO Theatre, which deals exclusively in such plays.

Tracey's show had a funny and disturbing premise. Her protagonist loses one hand in a car accident. The guy in the other car has been killed, and the surgeons mistakenly attach his hand to her arm. The hand is still conscious and still male, and it takes a sexual interest in her. Happy ending, in case you find this premise upsetting: she and the hand fall in love, get married, and waltz off together. Tracey called her play *Two Hander: A One Woman Show*.

In rehearsal, it became clear that the character she was creating and playing was not the ideal character for this story. Tracey herself was, and is, brave, bold, assertive, and adventurous, and she was devising her character along similar lines. But we decided that although even a character like that would be thrown for a loop by finding a man's hand attached to her arm, the stakes could be still higher if the character were prudish, timid, and solitary, and thus more threatened when the hand came alive. So this is an example of starting with a plot, and shaping the character to enhance the plot.

An example of starting with a character, and shaping the plot to fit the character, is Kevin Loring's play *Where the Blood Mixes*, about Floyd, a First Nations widower who reluctantly gave up his daughter to be adopted and raised by non-Indigenous people, and who is awaiting her coming to visit him now that she's an educated young woman.

Kevin knew that the reunion with his daughter would be the strongest challenge that Floyd could face, forcing him to confront the compromises and failures of his own life: an example of inventing a plot that will push a character to show what he's made of. The play began as a monologue in a Solo Show class, but when Kevin realized that Floyd needed a more active plot to challenge him, he evolved the play into a multi-character piece which went on to great success, including winning the Governor-General's Award for Drama.

The seven sources

The traditional sources for all fiction appear to be seven in number. If you can think of any more, write me. (Of course, the primary source of ideas is always your own imagination. But very often we create new work by blending elements derived from these sources.) So far, the list is as follows:

1. Mythology

2. History

3. Stories in the news

4. Stories about other people (i.e., anecdotes and gossip)

5. Stuff that's happened to you

6. Adaptation from other fiction

7. Plagiarism

Mythology

My first professionally produced play, a brief one-act called *Babel Rap*, is based on the Biblical story of the Tower of Babel (Genesis 11:1–9). As previously mentioned, my first full-length play was based on the myths about King Midas. In the 1940s, the French playwright Jean Anouilh wrote a modern version of the myth of Antigone, surrounding her with Nazis. George Bernard Shaw wrote a witty play based on the Ancient Roman story of Androcles and the Lion. Such Indigenous Canadian playwrights as Yolanda Bonnell, Waawaate Fobister, and the late Daniel David Moses have written startling modern versions of Indigenous myths. Ned Dickens has created a remarkable series of seven plays, *City of Wine*, based on the ancient Greek myths of Thebes. And the original classic plays of Greek and Roman mythology continue to be produced in translation. Mythology remains a draw, perhaps thanks to the contrast and tension between the mystical quality of these ancient cultures and the familiarity of their characters' emotions.

History

One of the biggest hits in Broadway history is Lin-Manuel Miranda's musical *Hamilton*, based on the life of the U.S. statesman. Another recent Broadway hit is *Come from Away* by Irene Sankoff and David Hein, a Canadian musical inspired by the aid given to American air passengers by the people of Gander, Newfoundland, during the World Trade Center attack in 2001. Toronto playwright

Michael Hollingsworth and his company Video Cabaret have invented a unique style in which they've created more than 20 satirical plays depicting eras of Canada's history, under the series title *The History of the Village of the Small Huts*. Arthur Miller's *The Crucible*, about the 17th-century Massachusetts witch hunts, was a brilliant response to the McCarthy Era. And, of course, our friend William's ten history plays have done passably well.

Stories in the news

Sometimes this kind of work is fictionalized, and sometimes it is explicitly a retelling of a news story.

My first successful full-length play, *Dreaming and Duelling* (1980), was fiction, inspired by an item in a Vancouver newspaper about two teenage boys in England who had tried to fight a duel to the death. Toronto playwright David S. Craig's TYA play *Danny, King of the Basement* (2001) was his response to the news that 25% of the homeless people in Toronto were children under the age of 12. (**TYA** stands for "Theatre for Young Audiences," the current term for theatre created by adult professionals, for audiences of children or teenagers.)

There are plays more explicitly based on specific news items. Colleen Murphy's acclaimed *Pig Girl* was a response to the horrific 2006 news stories about British Columbian Robert Pickton and his female murder victims, and her *The December Man* was inspired by the 1989 mass murder of 14 women at the Université de Montréal.

Anecdote and gossip, or stories you've heard about other people

My first produced play, *Chester, You Owe my Bird an Apology*, was inspired by a story a friend told me about a guy he knew who lived with his mother and hated her so much that he would torment her pet bird when she went out. My play *The Grandkid* was inspired by a friend's college-age daughter moving in with her grandfather, a prof at the university she was beginning to attend. Arthur Miller's *A View from the Bridge* is based on an anecdote a waterfront worker told him about a fellow worker.

STARTING TO START 39

Things that have actually happened to you

Autobiography, heavily or thinly disguised as fiction, is always a rich source of material, but has its pitfalls. Emotional Safety Warning: events you experienced some time ago can be useful, if they are now resolved or no longer hurt, but a crisis you're *currently* in may not be ideal playwriting material, at least for now. Of course, writing about it for yourself—"journaling"—is a time-honoured therapy technique. But you don't need the pressure of turning those messy problems into a script while also trying to solve them in real life.

If you do choose to write a play based on something that has happened to you, look at what it meant to you at the time, and at what it means to you now. What was the best thing about it, and what was the worst? Look for ways to raise the stakes. What if you, or someone else involved in the incident, had made different choices? How might things have become even more difficult?

Whether you publicly identify a play based on your experience as "autobiographical" is up to you. There's no strict definition. I'd advise against it, as it needlessly limits your choices of plot twists, and gets people speculating about you rather personally.

Adaptation

You may be asked, or may decide yourself, to write a stage adaptation of other fiction: a novel, a fairy tale, or another play written in another era, language, and/or culture.

There are legal and ethical questions around adaptation. The original work may be copyright. **Copyright** means the exclusive right to "copy" a document, i.e., to publish it or perform it publicly. Copyrights can be bought and sold, but by default it belongs to the author in the first place. (More about your own copyrights in Chapter 16.) Copyrights can also be inherited, but 70 years after the copyright owner's (usually the author's) death, the copyright expires, and the work goes into the **public domain**, which means it belongs to everyone.[16] So you can usually do what you want with a literary work by a long-dead author, but if you

16 There are exceptions. It gets complicated. There are books and websites on copyright law.

want to adapt a work by a writer who is still alive or has been dead for fewer than 70 years, you must get permission from the writer or their estate.

So let's assume you've secured the rights, or that it's a public-domain work. Different adaptations make different demands, depending on both the source and the intended result. An "adaptation" might be little more than a translation from a foreign language, sometimes with extra changes thrown in; or it can move a play from one time and place to another.

The first problem you're likely to encounter is the mundane question of length. When Toronto's Young People's Theatre asked me, in 1993, to adapt Hans Christian Andersen's fairy tale *The Nightingale* into a full-length play, the first challenge was to expand his 10-minute bedtime story into a two-hour entertainment. So I added more plot to the plot, rather than simply padding out the dialogue, and tried to do it so that viewers who didn't know the original could not tell where Andersen left off and I took over.

By contrast, when the St. Lawrence Shakespeare Festival of Prescott, Ontario asked me to adapt William's comedy *The Merry Wives of Windsor*, setting it in Prescott in the early 1900s and retitling it *Trouble on Dibble Street* (2010), there was cutting to do. *Merry Wives*, reportedly written in a hurry in response to a royal command from Queen Elizabeth I, contains an unresolved half-plot on top of his two complete plots, so that had to go. And the Festival is an outdoor summer theatre, so there was a strict time limit on length, to get to the curtain call before the nocturnal insects started feasting on the audience and actors.

Writing an adaptation means constantly deciding how closely you stick to the original and how much you make it your own play. (This can be expressed in the title and credit. Are you calling it by the original title, by the original author, adapted by you? Or is it a new title, written by you, adapted from the other guy?) These questions can only be answered by experience, but I will say that the more of these I've done, the freer I feel to muck with the original.

Adaptations can be as challenging as writing your own from scratch—or refreshingly *easier* than writing your own from scratch. Either way, it's fascinating to poke around inside another writer's work for a while. Sometimes you even get the lovely feeling that they're reading along over your shoulder and you're collaborating with greatness.

Plagiarism

Don't.

A cautionary note about writing real people

If your play is inspired by news stories, heard anecdotes, or your own life, it will include characters based on real people, perhaps from among your family or friends. Never use real names, or unique characteristics that could identify a person beyond any doubt. Besides hurting people's feelings, you could get sued.

If you know the real people personally, then it's up to you whether to tell them. Again, it's your call, but I'd advise you not to. It's not unethical to keep those secrets to yourself, and it's surprising how seldom people recognize their onstage selves. That might not be their fault, as it's as tricky to write an accurate likeness of a real person as it is to draw one. So that's another argument against telling people they're in your play: you add for yourself the difficult, unnecessary task of getting them "right."

And yet one more argument is that your characters' real-life counterparts might feel that they now have a stake in the work. It makes it difficult to change a character trait if you have to negotiate with that character's self-appointed human representative. Negotiating with the characters in your head is hard enough.

There are even dangers when the people you're writing about are deceased. You may feel inhibited in writing about people you love *especially* if they're gone. In recent years there have been some new Canadian plays publicly acknowledged to be about the playwrights' deceased parents. The plays have in common that the parent characters are rather unbelievably saintly. It is (truly) a touching display of filial affection, but it does deprive the characters of much of what might make them interesting.

Full disclosure: me too. *Homework & Curtains* (1991) was inspired by the death of my mother, whose fictional representative in the play is something of a paragon of virtue. In my opinion, the character's near-saintliness weakened the play. It would also have really ticked my mother off. (As always, there are exceptions: Michel Tremblay's plays about his family, notably *For the Pleasure of Seeing Her Again [Encore un fois, si vous permettez]*, 1998, about his deceased mother, are triumphs.)

Establishing the stakes

> You're so mean!
> —Queen's University playwriting student, when
> I suggested that, instead of a head cold, he give
> one of his characters cancer

The **stakes** are what you'd expect the word to mean: simply how important the situation is for the characters. You will keep adjusting the stakes throughout the writing of the play, but I'm putting this section here because setting them up in the first place is an important part of getting started.

Manipulating the stakes is often a matter of looking for ways to make things worse, because early drafts often suffer from low stakes. (It's a defining characteristic of those chat plays.) Most of us have been raised to avoid conflict, and our plots can be influenced by this polite reluctance to make trouble. So look to raise the stakes and make things tougher for the characters.

Often you can do so—and do other interesting things with the plot—by thinking in opposites: what would happen if the characters went through Changes and made Choices that were opposite to the ones you've given them? I learned this from watching my mother pause in her painting, turn the picture upside-down, and look at it in the mirror.

Sometimes the stakes can be *too* high, or can *appear* too high, if not motivated. Not every play needs to be life-or-death. Teachers of fiction find it disheartening that so many students' stories end with **protagonists** committing suicide. Not every hero must sacrifice his life to make it a serious drama. Killing a character is a solemn undertaking and should be well motivated.

(The **protagonist** is the central character, who makes everything happen and/or to whom everything happens. A **hero** is a protagonist with specific traditional virtues: courage, kindness, intelligence, resourcefulness, skills, physical strength, and a tragic flaw. The **antagonist** is the protagonist's enemy.)

The stakes can be defined as What the Protagonist Wants. Put in that context, they often become obvious. In a mystery, they're about solving the crime; in a romance, they're about realizing that one is in love, and/or capturing the heart of the beloved; and so on. Stakes don't have to be very original. We humans generally all want pretty much the same things: they don't make for a very long list. It's how the characters pursue them that interests us.

The film director Alfred Hitchcock coined the term "McGuffin" for what's at stake for the characters. His point was that the object itself doesn't matter: the Maltese Falcon, Desdemona's handkerchief, the microfilm hidden in the wine bottle—we're not watching the object, we're watching the characters chasing it. Quentin Tarantino has a witty visual comment on this in his *Pulp Fiction* (1994), where the McGuffin is a briefcase whose interior glows whenever it's opened, but whose contents we never get to see—because they don't matter.

You may find comic or dramatic dividends in *contrasting* stakes, where the stakes are very high for one character and low or nonexistent for another. Often the contrast is due to a secret being kept by one of the characters, such as a crush on another character. In *Swollen Tongues* (1999), a romantic comedy in verse by Vancouver's Kathleen Oliver, Sonja, a dressmaker, is measuring Catherine, her client. Unbeknownst to Sonja, Catherine is madly in love with her, and has written poems about her and published them in book form under a male pen name. Sonja, familiar with the poems but unaware that Catherine is their author or she herself their subject, asks her to read some of them aloud.

CATHERINE: What? You want me to read you this?

SONJA: Oh, yes!
while I take measurements for your new dress.
And while you read, I'll dream that you are he
who penned these gorgeous syllables to me!

(Throughout the following speeches, Sonja is taking measurements and fitting a dress for Catherine, who is increasingly uncomfortable with the physical intimacy.) [17]

CATHERINE: *(Aside)* How near to truth her blithe fantasy hits!

SONJA: Hold still, Catherine! I can't tell if this fits...
The bust is much too big. It needs a dart...

CATHERINE: *(Aside.)* Her hands upon my breast! Be still my heart!

So the stakes are comfortably low for Sonja, who is doing a job she does every day and is good at, while they are through the roof for Catherine, who must now read her own very revealing love poems while being thoroughly and professionally handled by the woman she secretly adores.

On triggers and warnings

Drama instructors have noticed a recent trend for their students to be overly protective of their audience's mental and emotional well-being. Some of this derives from a welcome increase in information and concern about mental health in general, some from an equally welcome concern for the feelings of BIPOC and LGBTQ theatre-goers in particular, and some, perhaps, from the isolation imposed on all of us by the COVID pandemic in the few years before I'm writing this.

For whatever reason, there are currently trigger warnings being posted in lobbies and printed in programs for the most innocuous entertainments. Announcements are made before performances,

---

17   Oliver's stage direction, not mine.

pointing out the exits and reassuring the audience that mental health experts are in the lobby, waiting to heal you if you must run out of the theatre.

Emotional triggers resulting from trauma are a real phenomenon and deserve to be taken seriously. But part of the purpose of theatre is to give us a chance to exercise our emotions in a safe place. The ancient Athenians said that the purpose of tragedy is to purge our bad feelings by evoking horror and pity.

The point of this section for you as a playwright is to urge you not to censor your own material too rigidly, or be afraid of raising the stakes, out of a concern for your audience's sensitivities. It's your job to put them through emotional changes in sympathy with your characters' changes. They can make up their own minds in advance about whether to risk this experience. If the theatre's publicity department chooses to post trigger warnings, that's their decision, though you're free to argue with them. And people can find out plenty about the content of a play before they decide whether to attend.

Theme versus message, or: what are plays for?

The process of imitation comes naturally to humans from childhood on. In this, we are different from other species, because we are the most imitative animal, we learn our first lessons by imitating, and imitation gives us great pleasure. [...] So when we see artistic representations, it helps us to understand the real thing and to see how they correspond, and we say, perhaps, "Oh, I know that person!"
—Aristotle, *The Poetics*, circa 330 B.C.E.,
Chapter 4

The purpose of playing [...] both at the first and now, was and is, to hold, as 'twere, the mirror up to nature; to show virtue her own feature, scorn his own image, and the very age and body of the time his form and pressure.
—William Shakespeare, *Hamlet*, Act 3, Scene 2

Theatre brings to light the life of the human soul.
—Konstantin Stanislavski

SIX-YEAR-OLD GIRL: Is this play gonna teach us anything?

ME: No, it's just gonna tell you a story.

GIRL: Oh, good.
—Conversation before a performance of a TYA play, elementary school gymnasium, Vancouver, 1986

Aristotle, William, Stanislavski, and the young critic quoted above agree that the purpose of plays is to entertain us by showing us human behaviour under interesting circumstances. There is a widespread contrary opinion, that plays should teach us how to be better people; but plays really don't seem to be effective delivery systems for such lessons. Plays seem to be best at showing us human behaviour—and, rather than delivering messages, exploring **themes**.

I learned in high school, and maybe you did too, the sensible principle that there are four elements to a work of fiction: Plot, Characters, Setting, and Theme. The first three seem clear: the Plot is what happens; the Characters are the people who make the plot happen and/or to whom it happens; and the Setting is when and where it happens. But what is this mysterious abstract term, Theme? And is it the same thing as a message?

To answer the second question first: no. Exploring a theme and delivering a message are two different operations. Most plays usually contain some of both: I was hedging the truth when I reassured that little girl that my play wouldn't teach her anything. Whether it's a "message play" or a "theme play" is mostly a question of which one it *emphasizes*. Try to put the emphasis on exploring themes and asking questions, rather than delivering messages and teaching answers.

The theme can be summed up as a noun, while the message is a sentence with the word "should" in it. You tell a friend you've just seen a play, and she asks you what it's about. If it's a theme play, you might say, "It's about global warming," or "homophobia," or "how we feel about our pets." If it's a message play, you're more likely to say, "It's about how we have to stop global warming," or "how we shouldn't discriminate against queer people," or "how we ought to treat our pets well because they depend on us." *Have to. Shouldn't. Ought to.*

Almost inevitably, at least one of your characters shares your opinions and at least one disagrees with you. There's nothing wrong with that. But in message plays, the audience gets the message in the first five minutes and keeps getting hit over the head with it for the rest of the play. "Yes, okay, I got it, I'll quit contributing to global warming / yelling at queer people / lying to my dog, I'm sorry, please stop now." The characters representing the playwright's views are usually the protagonists, and typically young, hopeful, idealistic, optimistic, and intelligent, with quick comebacks and wise observations. The antagonists, who represent the opposing views, are often old fogeys: bigoted, corrupt, and not very bright.

The Stupid Villain is a staple of movies for children, satirical sketch comedy, and some political theatre. They can be amusing—we get to feel superior to them—but unfortunately, real villains are often intelligent, or at least hire intelligent advisers. If they were always as dimwitted in reality as in some fiction, it would be easier to get rid of them, and the world would be a nicer place. (Admittedly, there have been some spectacularly stupid but alarmingly successful real-life villains in the news lately, as I write this. Nevertheless, I stand by my argument.)

So try to write nuanced, complicated, interesting antagonists— but know that doing so can lead you to an uncomfortable place. If you're writing about a subject you feel passionate about, such as racism, then ironically, *because* you hate racism, you must explore how the racist character feels, what motivates him, and why he's convinced he's right. Some actor is going to have to play that role, so it's your job to go there first.

Not all antagonists are evil people. Sometimes they mean well. But you still must inhabit the characters you disagree with. It helps if you have some sympathy for your antagonist(s), give them strong arguments, and treat your protagonist(s) with some healthy skepticism. It's rewarding to challenge your own assumptions while you're writing the play, and to have members of the audience arguing as they come out of the theatre.

As noted earlier, not all experts disapprove of Author's Messages. Lajos Egri, a Hungarian-American playwright, wrote *The Art of Dramatic Writing* (originally *How to Write a Play*, Simon & Schuster, 1942), considered a classic among playwriting books. He insisted that the playwright must begin with, and must believe in, their play's "Premise"—which sounds an awful lot like an Author's Message: his suggested "premises" include "Bitterness leads to false gaiety," "Foolish generosity leads to poverty," "Honesty defeats duplicity," etc.

Of course, you're free to read Egri's book and others, and make up your own mind. But before you do, let's look at four of the most famous plays ever written as if they were message plays, designed to teach us how to behave if we're ever in the protagonist's situation:

If *Hamlet* has a message, it is that if a supernatural creature comes to you and asks you to go kill the King, go right downstairs and kill the King. Don't wander around the castle pretending you're crazy, scaring your girlfriend, putting on plays and yelling at your mother—just go kill the King. Because if you wait too long, then a lot of other people—namely your mother, your girlfriend, your girlfriend's father, your girlfriend's brother, two guys you went to school with, and you—will die as well.

The message of *Macbeth* is that if supernatural creatures come to you and imply that you might want to kill the King, don't do it. It's a trap.

If *A Midsummer-Night's Dream* has a message, it is, don't go into the woods at night, because there are fairies. Fairies are real, they are dangerous, amoral, and powerful, and they're liable to mess with your head—in Nick Bottom's case, literally. Beware of fairies!

The message of *The Merry Wives of Windsor* is: don't be an idiot, there's no such thing as fairies, and if people know you believe in them, everybody in town will laugh at you.[18]

---

18 To be fair, that last one's a bit of a stretch. The real message of *Merry Wives* is, if you want to seduce two different people, first find out if they're friends

And yet all four of these plays were written by the same guy![19] Had he no consistency? No, he had no consistency, because these plays were set in different worlds. (The **world** of a play is its reality, the collection of natural laws in which it is set.) In the world of *Hamlet*, "It is an honest Ghost;"[20] in the world of *Macbeth*, the Witches are "juggling fiends"[21] who "tell us truths, / Win us with honest trifles, to betray's / In deepest consequence."[22] In the fantasy world of *A Midsummer-Night's Dream*, fairies are real; in the homespun, cheerfully mundane, realistic Windsor of *Merry Wives*, they are not.

So if we look at these as message plays whose purpose is to teach us how to behave when we meet ghosts, fairies, and precognitive witches, they are useless. But if we look at them as plays that explore themes and hold the mirror up to human nature, by showing us Characters facing Challenges, going through Changes, and making Choices, well, these are four darn fine plays.

and then don't send them the same love letter. (Of the messages offered here, this one stands the best chance of being of some practical use.)

19 Shakespeare, William, 1564–1616.

20 Act I, Scene 5.

21 Act V, Scene 8.

22 Act I, Scene 3.

3

Originality, Appropriation, and Research

Originality

The man who writes about himself and his own time is the only man who writes about all people and all time. [23]
—George Bernard Shaw

We are the most narrated-to generation in history. There are more stories told to us every day than to any generation before us. In the 19th century, a family might enjoy a chapter or two of a novel in the evening before bed, and that was their daily allotment of narrative. But today, between commercials, news items, books, newspapers, magazines, movies and series on TV or streaming services, movies in theatres, and let's not forget plays, we consume a larger number of stories of varying sizes in a day than our ancestors did in a month—from the moment we wake up and turn on Facebook until we turn off YouTube and go to sleep.

---

23 Yes: sexist. Sorry about that, but it's a highly relevant comment, so I've included it. Let's pretend he wrote "writer" or "person." Writing "man" may be surprising, coming from a feminist sympathizer like Shaw, but he was a bundle of contradictions, and also, like all of us, a product of his time.

In 1973, the American literary critic Harold Bloom wrote a book called *The Anxiety of Influence*, about the pressure we feel from the existence of great works of the past. With such a history of masterpieces behind us, and great writers looking over our shoulders, how do we come up with anything new? It's all been done, we tell ourselves (or well-meaning others tell us). All the stories have been told!

Well, maybe and maybe not, but they haven't been told by *you*. Perhaps your best chance at originality as a playwright is to write work based on the real people around you, rather than on other writers' writings. If you use your own takes on the behaviour, politics, morality, slang, speech rhythms, fads and fashions of the people in your life, your work will be original. If you base it on somebody else's latest movie / podcast / TV show / livestream, then it won't. Trust your instincts, your obsessions, and your own sense of observation, and get creative with them to write what you see and hear in your world.

In my classes I forbid parody, pastiche, and political or social satire featuring caricatures of public figures. The characters and situations have to be creations of the students, inspired by real people like those the students see and hear around them.

Here's another rule you might want to adopt. A student was writing a play about the "real" relationship between Jesus and Judas, but we never got very far into that intriguing premise, because we got hung up on the style of dialogue. Should they speak in Early-17th-century King-James-Bible-style English, all "thee" and "thou"? Or in present-day English, but formally? Or present-day slang? We got so stuck on this issue that we barely got to work on the play itself. So I instituted a rule that the students' plays must take place during their lifetimes, and either in our society or in one they have lived in.

Sorry if it sounds condescending, but that's a good idea for beginners. The rule was used in my "Introduction to Playwriting" course, but I relaxed it in the more advanced courses. With age and experience you may find it rewarding to try breaking this rule, if you enjoy writing dialects and feel confident about it. But be warned that nothing looks more amateurish than inaccurate dialect. If you write a dialect that you do not regularly speak, assume that somebody who *does* regularly speak like that will read or see your play. We'll have a little more to say about the issue of appropriation later in this chapter.

One more rule that might be of interest, which arose from those concerns outlined in the previous chapter about the pitfalls of writing about real people: the students are free to base their characters on people they know, and their situations on actual incidents—but they are *forbidden to tell us* if that's the case. We treat the work as pure fiction, even if we're privately convinced that it's about the students' family or friends. (And there have been times when I've later learned that I was wrong to assume the student's story was true.)

Two questionable takes on originality

There are numerous theories to the effect that there are only 36 "dramatic situations," or 20 "master plots," or 13 "ways of looking at the novel," or seven "basic stories." These lists seem awfully reductive. It makes more sense, and is certainly more encouraging, to assume that there are trillions of basic stories: several hundred for each human on the planet. However, if you find these lists helpful, more power to you, and if you write one or more plays based on them, then break a leg[24] on opening night and have a great success.

Another apparent enemy to originality is those computer programs designed to help you create your plot and characters (not to be confused with formatting programs, which are useful, though some programs combine the two functions). I admit that in condemning these, I'm in danger of mistrusting a trend because I don't know anything about it because I mistrust it. And as Artificial Intelligence evolves, as it is currently doing by leaps and bounds, it promises to become more and more difficult to distinguish from human creativity, so this section may start to look very obsolete, very soon. News stories have begun to appear, describing some

---

24 "Break a leg" is theatre artists' way of wishing each other good luck with a show.

theatre companies, such as England's Young Vic, using A.I. to help them write plays.[25]

However, for now, if some current movies and TV shows look as if they were written by computers, it may be because they were. When A.I. begins to develop emotions to the point where computers begin to enjoy reading or watching fiction, then it will make sense to have plays written for them by other computers. But for human audiences, it still makes more sense to have plays written by humans. And perhaps the best argument against having a computer program do your playwriting for you is, to borrow John Cleese's favourite line from *Monty Python's Flying Circus*, "Where's the pleasure in that?"[26]

Appropriation: the predicament

As of this writing, the issue of cultural appropriation is one of the hottest topics in the arts. It's a small part of a long-overdue revolution in how we all treat each other. Old habits of sexism, racism, ageism, homophobia, transphobia, and ableism are breaking down, let's hope, and people who once suffered in silence while one particular group told everybody else's stories are now taking charge of their own stories, to everyone's benefit.

I've come up with an acronym for that group who used to tell everybody else's stories—the demographic I myself belong to: Straight (Cisgender, Heterosexual), Male, Old, and White—which gives us SCHMOWs. I hereby decree that the word must be pronounced with a long O, which, by a convenient coincidence, makes it sound just like "schmo," a Yiddish word meaning a dull, stupid or boring person.[27]

---

25   https://www.theguardian.com/stage/2021/aug/24/rise-of-the-robo-drama-young-vic-creates-new-play-using-artificial-intelligence

26   https://www.timeout.com/film/john-cleese

27   Firstly, I don't consider it an act of cultural appropriation for a non-Jewish person to make a pun on a Yiddish word, and secondly I'm Jewish, so, in the words of my people, don't hock mir a chynik.

Until recently it has been almost exclusively my fellow Schmows who have told the stories of just about everybody else, and quite a botch of the job we have done too. There are scathing books and film documentaries about how badly our fiction has represented indigenous North Americans, African-Americans, and LGBTQ people—and everywhere we look, we see demeaning ways that men depict women.

So it is understandable that non-Schmows are now saying, "Okay, thank you, Schmows, you can step aside now, we'll take it from here." And the results are good for us all, with a current explosion of exciting new work from fresh perspectives. If, as a side effect, there is a reduction of opportunities for us traditionally over-privileged Schmows, it would be churlish to complain about it, after having had the field pretty much to ourselves for centuries.

But on the other hand, fiction is appropriation. By definition. To write fiction is to appropriate other people's reality: to say, "I don't know what it's like to be you, but I'm going to imagine it." If we were suddenly forbidden to write about people we were not, then each demographic's fictional efforts would fill up with nothing but fellow members of that demographic. Fiction—and biography, autobiography and history—would become impossible.

So two political and aesthetic questions arise out of these concerns: where do we draw the line, and who gets to draw it?

Appropriation: a solution

Happily, as this is being written in the early 2020s, a reasonable consensus appears to be emerging. It says that we all, including us Schmows, may continue to write fiction, and that, as always, the writer gets to draw the line where the writer chooses. But now there is a principle which changes everything for the better: a very firm demand that we write *with respect for, and in direct consultation with, the people about whose demographic we're writing.*

This view is being put forward not just by the Schmows but also by some persuasive people from other demographics. Among them, the Indigenous playwright and essayist Drew Hayden Taylor wrote an opinion piece in the *Globe and Mail* in 2020, with the headline *Indigenous characters belong in non-Native literature too, as long as they are written with respect.* In it, he wrote:

> I think it would be a travesty if Native characters were completely wiped out of non-Native Canadian literature. We're far too interesting a people and have contributed way too much to this contemporary society. [...] Just do your research. [...] If your character is going to be Native, make him Native for a reason and support it. I do the same for my non-Native characters. Talk to people in our community. Take an elder out for tea. Go to a First Nation to ask a question and buy a T-shirt. We want to be in your books. [...] But perhaps one of the most important of the seven Grandfather teachings, which much of my Anishinawbe culture and many others rely upon, says it all: Respect. If you're putting one of us in your book to make money, just keep moving. If you're putting one of us in your book as a sign of respect, pull up a chair.[28]

Other writers who are not straight, white men have contributed to this view. Among them, Samia Rahman, a Muslim journalist living in England, has written advice on "How to Write the 'Other' (Without Being a Jerk)," and the Vancouver Latinx theatre artist, memoirist, and social activist Carmen Aguirre recorded a video essay in 2021 passionately rejecting the "cancel culture" that sometimes arises as a response.

The current recommended way to write about members of demographics to which you yourself do not belong is, as Taylor suggests above, by inviting friends and acquaintances who belong to the demographic(s) that you're writing about—ideally, but not necessarily, fellow theatre people—to read your work in progress and give you feedback. (And if you don't have friends and acquaintances outside your own demographic, get some, and not just for the good of your play.)

---

28 https://www.theglobeandmail.com/arts/books/article-indigenous-characters-belong-in-non-native-literature-too-as-long-as/

Such consultants are called **sensitivity readers**. Like other dramaturges, whose work we'll discuss in Chapter 14, they should be paid, or otherwise reimbursed, for their time and effort. And their advice can be invaluable, saving you from great embarrassment or worse.

Research

> The highest form of research is essentially play.
> —N. V. Scarfe, who attributed it
> to Albert Einstein

This obligation to consult leads us to the larger topic of research. If you're one of those whose eyes don't light up at that word, be assured that researching your play can be one of the most enjoyable parts of the writing. Often it consists in immersing yourself in the culture of a different period or society. This kind of research can offer great, fascinating stimulation, partly thanks to its randomness and surprises. Besides, if you're a self-employed artist, even part-time, then what you do spend can be deducted from your income tax!

You may, while watching a video of an Oscar-winning Hollywood screenwriter to see how he uses plot cards, stumble across a great quotation from him about how stories can change the world.[29] The film reviews of Pauline Kael might lead you to the plays of Lillian Hellman, and the memoirs of Lillian Hellman might lead you to the writings of Dashiell Hammett. The essays of Suzan-Lori Parks might lead you to the plays of Lorraine Hansberry; Maurice Sendak might lead you to Mozart; Irishman Oscar Wilde's touring North America with a Black valet might lead you to the tensions between African-Americans and Irish immigrants in 1880s New York City. Such open-ended research is indeed one of the more creative and enjoyable parts of the process.

---

29 This is not hypothetical, though my research was not for a play but for a playwriting course. The screenwriter is Dustin Lance Black, and the video is at https://www.youtube.com/watch?v=vrvawtrRxsw. The other examples given here are also from my own real experience.

PART 2

THE TWO WAYS:
PLOT AND DIALOGUE

4

Plot, the Theory

Climaxes, Cause-and-Effect, Etc.

Plotting is fun! (though not everyone agrees)

A play is a series of *contrivances*, which—frightfully sorry—must be *contrived*.

—Sir Laurence Olivier

Now we're getting down to how to build a plot. Occasionally you'll come across a writer who seems not to need to know this, but who claims to just plunge in at the beginning, writing the work in detail, with no idea where the plot is going to go—and yet somehow it develops elegantly on its own. If you share that intuitive talent, congratulations, and you may choose to skip these next few chapters, or at least until such time as you lose your confidence. For the rest, here is one tried-and-true method for building a plot.

As hinted before, it involves outlines. Sometimes, wrong-headed ideas lead to rewarding results, and I'm glad my 29-year-old self had the notion, expressed in the Introduction, that writing plot outlines would be boring. That mistake led to the "compromise" of alternating between plot and dialogue, and to seeing them as the two sides of the process. It was then an unexpected bonus to discover that the plotting could also be an enjoyable activity, after all.

In fairness, some writers disagree. One renowned playwright told me privately that to her, "plotting is like hard math." Others find plots easy to write (or so they say), but of little interest. Oscar Wilde said, "Plots are tedious. Anyone can invent them. Life is full of them. Indeed, one has to elbow one's way through them as they crowd across one's path."[30]

Chat plays

People who read and watch plays for a living have encountered their fair share of those chat plays mentioned in Chapter 1. A friend, after judging a playwriting contest, summed them up well: "There was a tremendous tendency for nothing to happen." Some playwrights seem to think live theatre *should* be boring: that it is *meant* to be all talk and no action. Pauline Kael once referred to people who believe that being bored in the theatre is good for you. It isn't. It's just boring.

Chat plays remind us, by omission, that everything should happen for two reasons. In those plays, the characters' needs are met: it's pleasant to sit around with friends, discussing stuff. But it's not of much interest to the audience, because the storyteller's needs are not being met: there's no story to keep us hooked. However, if the audience were to know that, say, one of the characters was hiding a bomb under the table, then you'd have their attention. (That image is borrowed from Canadian playwright and teacher Judith Thompson, who tells her students, "Find the bomb under the play.") Plot shows the characters at their most exciting, and gives the play structure, logic, and engaging, satisfying action.

It can be helpful to construct much of your plot separately from the process of writing your dialogue. My mother spoke of an art student painting the leaves on a tree in a corner of the canvas, without having sketched in the rest of the landscape—a painter's equivalent to scribbling dialogue without knowing where the plot is going. Later, the tree proved to be out of proportion and had to be repainted, and all that detail work was lost. Her own approach was to keep all parts of the canvas at roughly the same level of

---

30   Hesketh Pearson, *Oscar Wilde: His Life and Wit,* (New York and London: Harper & Brothers).

development at any given time. These chapters are about how to achieve the playwright's equivalent to keeping the whole canvas evolving at once.

The Guide Sentence

It can be very useful to have a one-sentence summation of your basic plot. Write one early on. You can change it later, as many times as you need to, as your play progresses. If anybody ever turns to you in a workshop or in rehearsal and says, "So what's the central action in this play?" or, "What's this play about?' you can resort to your Guide Sentence.

It doesn't have to reveal the entire plot, but it should cover the basic situation. For example, a Guide Sentence for *Macbeth* might read, "An army officer is persuaded, by three witches and his wife, to kill the King and take over the throne, but then becomes a tyrant, and the people rise up against him." The Guide Sentence for *Totally Nana's Ride*, the 10-minute play in Chapter 6, is (sorry, spoiler alert, but you're not the audience, you're here to learn stuff): "A young woman finds her long-lost grandmother's car, learns that her boyfriend has been unfaithful to her in that same car, and buys the car, offering the boyfriend as part of the purchase price."

I call it a Guide Sentence partly because it's a guide to the play, and partly in honour of *TV Guide*, the pre-Internet magazine that offered weekly local schedules of television programs, with a sentence describing each program. There's an old joke about a *TV Guide* writer who is asked to knock off a sentence for a movie of *Hamlet*, and who, having perhaps seen too many soap operas, writes, "College boy, home for the holidays, has trouble adjusting to new stepfather."[31] Though just a joke, this makes the point that a Guide Sentence can be an interpretation, and can suggest an attitude to the material: you could direct a production of *Hamlet*

---

31 The late David French's 1980 backstage comedy *Jitters* is about a theatre company producing a play with the exquisitely 1950s title *The Care and Feeding of Roses*. That play-within-the-play is about a college boy, home for the holidays, who's having trouble adjusting to his new stepfather. I've always wondered if French was inspired by that joke.

based on this premise. It might be a rather odd production, but you could do it.

The plot begins: interrupting a routine

Conventionally, a play begins with a status quo, which gets interrupted by a usually minor complication: the first Challenge to the Character. That first interruption has been described as "a cloud as small as a man's hand."[32] From there, the plot will thicken, as the Characters go through the Changes and make the Choices that give rise to further Challenges.

The late, great master of improvisation Keith Johnstone used to say that improvisers should not stand onstage trying to make up stories but should think instead in terms of *interrupting routines*. This principle arose in the context of improvisation but is very helpful to playwrights. Most plots can be looked at as a series of routines, which become interrupted by new plot developments, thus creating new routines. Those chat plays might be defined as plays that show us the routine without the interruption.

Another way to think about the process of repeatedly interrupting routines comes to us from philosopher Georg Hegel. He was describing historical events and philosophical arguments, but this model applies as easily to the creating and developing of plots. Hegel writes of three stages. First there's the *thesis*, the status quo, the routine. Then it's confronted by an *antithesis*—a rebellion, a counter-argument, an interruption in the routine—and then the two grapple with each other, through Changes and Choices—and evolve into a *synthesis*, which forms the new thesis until the next argument or revolution comes along.[33]

On climaxes and dénouements

The plot customarily then builds to a **climax**: the moment when the plot reaches its highest level of stress and is resolved, as the

---

32 The phrase is taken from I Kings 18:44.

33 Although this idea is almost universally attributed to Hegel, he himself claimed it originated with his fellow philosopher Immanuel Kant.

protagonist either completes or fails to complete the central task. Hamlet kills Claudius. Frodo throws the ring into the fire. The climax of Alice Walker's novel *The Color Purple* (1982) is the reunion of the sisters. The climax of *Cinderella* is when the shoe fits.

Sometimes when the word "climax" is spoken in writing classes, there's giggling over the sexual meaning. (The stereotype is that this happens in high schools, but I've heard more snickering in classes of senior citizens.) To address this head-on: yes, it's a human thing. Sex features climaxes, traditionally. So does childbirth. So do some arguments, competitions, fights, and deaths. It seems there's something in us humans that wants to be led up to that climax, so it comes in handy in theatre.

Often there will be one last major setback before the climax: that moment when the audience just doesn't know how the hero is going to get out of this fix. In some versions of *Cinderella*, the Prince is about to leave with the slipper without knowing Cinderella is locked in the cellar. In *The Lord of the Rings*, Frodo can resist the pull of the Ring no longer, and puts it on. In many thrillers, the hero is tied up in the lair of the villain, who is going to kill him just as soon as he finishes his gloating explanation of the plot thus far. But then, of course, Cinderella is released, Frodo loses both ring and finger, the hero rallies, and the climax is achieved.

After it comes the **dénouement**, which traditionally wraps up the loose ends, shows us the characters enjoying some peace at last, restores the original routine or establishes a new one, and/ or suggests a fresh conflict on the horizon. Some plots have no dénouement but place the climax at the very last word. This effect is comparatively rare in theatre, but it does turn up in many short stories and the occasional play, like *The Inspector-General* (1836) by Nikolai Gogol, or the one-act play *The Monkey's Paw* (1907) by Louis N. Parker, from the horror story by W.W. Jacobs.

Here is a rough graph of how the excitement might build in a one-act play. The squiggles are approximations of moments where the excitement increases or plot complications are introduced.

Suggested Structure for a One-Act Play

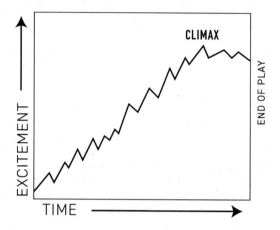

Below is a similar graph for a two-act play. ("Acts" and "scenes" are defined in Chapter 12.) It helps to have a sub-climax at the end of each act, which does not resolve the conflict, but may introduce a new crisis, and keeps the audience wondering how it will end. I call this "bringing them back from the bar."

Suggested Structure for a Two-Act Play

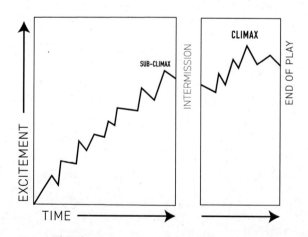

Finally on this subject: there's a different model of plot structure, used as long ago as Aristotle's time (4th Century B.C.E.), with a different definition of "climax." Among other places it appears in Richard Greenblatt's *Text and Context: The Operative Word*, first mentioned in our Introduction.

Greenblatt defines the "climax" as "the event that irreparably changes the world of the characters," and, following Aristotle, places it about three-fifths of the way through the play, calling everything before that point "rising action" and everything after it "falling action."[34] According to this view, the climax of *Hamlet* would be the death of Polonius in Act 3, not the deaths of Claudius and Hamlet at the end.

I'm mentioning the Aristotle / Greenblatt model here in the name of fairness, and to prevent confusion if you find it elsewhere. The two models do seem to contradict each other, and yet somehow they co-exist in the same space-time continuum, and Richard and I remain friends.

Building a plot with Cause-and-Effect

> When I come up with ideas, they'll just start from a very, like, primal, "I just wanted to see this cute thing onscreen," and then I'll find the meaning and the metaphor and the themes to justify why it should be that. But really it just came from a place of, like, "Ah, that's so cute! And wouldn't it be awesome if they were gigantic!"
> —Domee Shi, writer and director of the feature film *Turning Red* (Pixar, 2022), interviewed in the featurette *Embrace the Panda*

This section describes one way to build a plot. There are others, but if you learn this one, then you can do it other ways too. Also, this approach works pretty consistently.

Once you've decided what you want to write about, start thinking about moments you'd like to see in your play. They can be grand and glorious or small and simple. They can be confrontations, exchanges or single lines of dialogue, moments of onstage action, special effects—anything that makes you think, "Yeah, this could

34 *Text and Context*, 48.

be funny," or "This might hit them hard," or, as Domee Shi says above, "Ah, that's so cute!"

Start writing them down, in any order. Fill a few pages with such ideas: visuals, moments of dialogue, character descriptions. If you draw, then draw some characters, sets or costumes. Get your brain daydreaming about this play you want to see. Give it a working title. (More about titles in Chapter 11.) You can do all this on literal paper pages in a notebook or sketchbook devoted to your new play, or in a computer file called "Notes" in a new directory devoted to the play. (See "Keeping Organized for Yourself," Chapter 12.) Once you have some pages of these, the next step is to start linking up some of these different ideas by means of Cause-and-Effect.

Cause-and-Effect is the drive train of your plot, the secret potion, the magic trick that makes plotting happen. If you manage it well, the plot seems to unfold by itself and the audience doesn't know how you did it.

Put simply, you take those moments in your play and find ways that one moment can cause the next, and so on, in a chain. And that's it. It might seem straightforward and obvious, but it has infinite possibilities. It is best explained in more detail by using examples. You can trace how Cause-and-Effect is used in the plots of most works of fiction. Here are three, by Alan Ayckbourn, William Shakespeare, and the team of Joa Lazarus and me.

Cause-and-Effect in Relatively Speaking

One playwright who revels in the intricacies of plot construction is the great English writer of farce and comedy, Sir Alan Ayckbourn. Here he describes how he devised the ingenious opening scene of his 1965 play *Relatively Speaking*, in which Ginny and Greg are a young couple and Ginny is in a secret affair with a middle-aged married guy named Philip:

> Since the younger man, Greg, needed to meet both the older man, Philip, and his wife, Sheila, it made sense to set the piece in the older couple's house. All that was needed then was a contrivance to get the girl, Ginny, there as well. Perhaps she

was there finally to break off her relationship with Philip? Feasible. There were all sorts of problems presented by that, but it would do as an initial working plan. [...]

It was important that Greg arrived in the house convinced that it belonged to Ginny's parents. How does that come about? Obviously, she must have told him it does. Why should she do that? Because she's coming down to break off her relationship with Philip and doesn't want Greg to know where she's going. It's a spur-of-the-moment lie by her, to put the boyfriend off the scent.

Where does she tell him? We are going to need a pre-scene, a prologue before we can start the narrative rolling. With luck, this prologue could be used to serve more than one purpose. More anon.

But how does he get there, to the house? Answer: he follows her. But if he follows her, it means he must necessarily arrive second. And for the sake of the initial confusion of identity it's important that although she leaves first, so that he is convinced he's following her, in fact she is delayed so he arrives first. (The plotting is getting rather complicated.)[35]

But that means that Greg finds his way to the supposed parents' house without following her. Which means he already knows the address. How does he know the address? Because he finds it somewhere, written down in her flat, that's why. Which conveniently—wait for it—explains why Ginny tells him it's her parents' address. Which is not a very clever lie because why on earth should someone write down their parents' address? Which makes him suspicious, which is why he follows her. It's getting clearer.[36]

See what he does there? He doesn't use the term "Cause-and-Effect," but that technique informs all of his thinking. "*How* does that come about?" "*Why* should she do that? *Because*..." "But *how* does he get there, to the house?" "*so that* he is convinced..." "*so* he arrives

35 Ayckbourn's parenthetical comment, not mine.

36 Alan Ayckbourn, *The Crafty Art of Playmaking* (London: Faber and Faber, 2002), 12–14.

first…" "*How* does he know the address? *Because…*" "That's *why*." "Which conveniently—wait for it—explains *why…*" "*why* on earth …" "…which is *why* he follows her." (Emphases added, obviously.)

Cause-and-Effect in Hamlet

Let's revisit our friend Polonius, and, this time, his whole family. In the Scandinavian legends that William used as his source, "Amleth" does get involved with a young woman and does kill an intruder whom he mistakes for his evil uncle "Feng" (yeah, that's his name), but he's never met the intruder before, and the third member of the Polonius clan, Laertes, doesn't appear in the legends.

So let's imagine William sitting in the Mermaid Tavern, looking over his plot outline. He has the basics worked out and he wants three more characters. He wants to give Hamlet a girlfriend, as in the source material, and see how Hamlet treats her. Call her Ophelia. (For your info, in case you don't know the play, he treats her like dirt.) Then he needs Hamlet to kill the wrong guy, so that Claudius will send him to England and all that other stuff will happen: he'll call that unfortunate fellow Polonius. And finally, a young swordsman, call him Laertes, visits Elsinore and fights the duel with Hamlet, using a secretly sharpened and poisoned rapier. It would be cool to have Laertes in on the murder plot with Claudius, but William doesn't know yet how to motivate that, so for now he assumes the swordsman is an innocent pawn in Claudius' game.

These three might have had nothing to do with each other. Ophelia, in the tradition of girlfriends in plays written by men about men, could have been there just to worry about the hero. Polonius could have been some random stooge who snuck into Gertrude's bedroom to steal jewellery, hears her and Hamlet coming in, hides behind the arras and gets killed. And Laertes could have been a swordsman touring Europe who stops at Elsinore and is challenged to a friendly match with the Prince.

But William wants more out of these characters. Hey, what if they have connections of their own? Father, brother, and sister? And so he creates a subplot which is a small masterpiece of Cause-and-Effect.

Polonius worries that Hamlet might seduce and ruin his daughter, which causes him to tell her to break up with Hamlet. To cover up his plans to kill Claudius, Hamlet pretends he's mad,[37] which frightens Ophelia, causing her to tell her father, which causes him to decide that it's his own fault that the heir to the throne of Denmark has gone nuts—over Ophelia dumping him on Polonius' orders—which causes him to hide behind the arras in Gertrude's bedroom. Hamlet frightens Gertrude, which causes her to shout, which causes Polonius to shout, which causes Hamlet to kill him.

And this murder causes pretty much everything else in the play. It causes Claudius to send Hamlet to England; Ophelia to go mad; Laertes to come home from Paris in time to see his sister gone mad; and Ophelia to drown herself. And now Laertes is fully caused—or, you might say, motivated—to join Claudius in planning to murder Hamlet. (You can often substitute the word "motivate" for the word "cause," as in this sequence: after all, it's the characters' motivations that cause their choices.)

Cause-and-Effect in Dreaming and Duelling

Dreaming and Duelling emerged after *Midas*, from the decision to develop a plot outline while writing the dialogue. The play was suggested by an item in a Vancouver paper about two English teenage boys who tried to fight a duel to the death over a girl. What first inspired the play was the image of two present-day teenagers—we named them Joel and Eric—in jeans and T-shirts and running shoes, up to their knees in dry-ice vapour, engaged in grand, romantic swordfights. So the play began life with nothing more than a cool visual, like Domee Shi's cute giant panda.

Joa and I gathered ideas for moments that might be good to have in the play. The late director Jace Van Der Veen suggested that the play contain duelling sequences of different kinds—playful, studious, or in deadly earnest—like production numbers in a musical. This brilliant idea paved the way for the discovery described below. We

---

37 This plot point has given rise to hundreds of years of arguing over whether Hamlet is "genuinely" mad or just faking it. I find this a weird question. He's not "genuinely" anything. He's a fictional character.

proceeded with various other ideas for moments, gathered in no particular order, including these three:

1. When I was a student at the National Theatre School, we were in the locker room after a fencing class one day, and a student asked another student to explain a new move which he hadn't understood. The other guy took two wire clothes hangers, untwisted them, straightened them out, gave one to his friend, and said, "Okay, so if I come at you like this…" and the two of them replicated the move in slow motion, while the rest of us watched. It was not a moment of high drama, but it was kind of neat, and had stuck in my head, and now I thought might serve as one of the duelling sequences Jace had suggested.

2. It seemed almost obligatory that either Joel or Eric argue with the fencing teacher in her office. Arguing with teachers in offices had been a recurring feature of my own high school life, and reportedly that of many other people, and seemed a natural choice.

3. This one had the potential to be a central part of the plot: Skelly, the class bully, insults the boys' friend Louise. Joel, defending her honour, challenges Skelly to a duel. Skelly, in the duelling tradition, chooses the weapons—Joel and Eric's épées—figuring he'll show what a great athlete he is by beating Joel at his own sport, which Skelly's never tried before. Joel beats the daylights out of him.

Then the light bulb went on: one of these three moments could cause the next moment, which in turn could cause the third moment.

Joel challenges Skelly, they pick up the épées, Joel disarms Skelly and is about to slash him across the face, when Mrs. Thorpe, the fencing teacher, comes up behind him and grabs his épée. Joel hollers an obscenity, turns around and sees that he's shouted the F word at the teacher, and the buzzer goes for the end of class and the end of Act One (an example of the principle mentioned earlier of "bringing them back from the bar").

This of course causes the argument between Joel and Mrs. Thorpe in her office, as the opening of Act Two. But then something new popped up. Clearly, the only plausible response Mrs. Thorpe could have to Joel's outrageous, unsafe behaviour is to expel him from fencing class. This gave us a new link in the chain. It causes Joel to come to the locker room after the next class and demand that Eric show him what he learned that day, which causes the wire-hangers scene.

As we wrote the wire-hangers scene, it became clear how much Joel's expulsion from fencing class gave to the story. Fencing is the main thing Joel lives for. So the wire-hangers scene has Joel in a state of desperation, and also has Eric angry at Joel for depriving Eric of his valued fencing partner, and resentful at now having to update him after each class.

Cause-and-Effect: summing up and moving on

In case these three examples are a little confusing, as they use Cause-and-Effect to illustrate three different purposes, here's a summing-up:

In *Relatively Speaking*, Ayckbourn had one particular moment he wanted to see—Greg meeting the older couple and thinking they are Ginny's parents—and used Cause-and-Effect very skillfully to bring that moment about.

In *Hamlet*, William appears to have taken three minor characters who impinge on the main plot in different ways, made them into a family, and used Cause-and-Effect to craft their own little tragic subplot: a sort of service road, which meets up with the main road at different points in the play.

And in *Dreaming and Duelling*, the insertion of one more link into the chain of Cause-and-Effect—Joel's expulsion from fencing class— raised the stakes and heightened the emotion of the wire-hangers scene, and of the whole play: an example of the kinds of gifts that can turn up unexpectedly when you're busy with Cause-and-Effect.

But how do playwrights actually, physically *do* this? What does this organization of Cause-and-Effect look like in practice? Well, there are many techniques. One is a way of laying out the sequences in a useful sort of diagram, made of index cards. And this calls for a chapter of its own.

5

Plot, the Practice

Playing your Cards Right

Let's deal the cards

The tools introduced here for plot construction are simple, but their very simplicity makes them hugely useful and infinitely versatile. They're just a deck of blank, three-by-five or four-by-six index cards, a felt marker with a medium-sized nib, and a large table. You write different moments for your play, each on its own card, in the simplest words possible, in big, clear, black block letters; lay them all out on the table; and push them around to get them into the order you want. And that's it.

(This is just one technique among many for controlling the process of developing plot. Other popular approaches include "clustering," and a technique that the American writer Randy Ingermanson calls the "Snowflake Method," in which, as with a snowflake, more and more detail accretes to the plot as it "crystalizes.")

Of course, none of this is mandatory! As suggested earlier, you may have such a clear sense of your plot that you can simply start writing dialogue and adjust the plot as necessary if and when it starts to go off the rails. However, many writers before me have found the index-card technique useful over the years, so here it is.

1. You know those moments that you decided you'd like to have in your play, back in the previous chapter, under "Building a Plot with Cause-and-Effect"? Take all the ones that describe plot and write each one on its own card. Also, now's a good time to think up others. The more, the merrier.

2. You may already know, or suspect, the order in which at least some of these plot points appear. Place them in that order on the table. It seems to work best to create vertical columns, with earliest stuff at the top and later stuff under it. Or some people like to work left-to-right.

3. For those cards whose order you don't know yet, try some out. *Think in terms of Cause-and-Effect.* How can this card cause that card? Or be caused by that other card? Or might this card cause, or be caused by, a new one that you haven't written yet? How would that new one read? How about if you wrote a new card and stuck it between these two, so that it is caused by the previous one and then causes the next one?

4. Muck around with them. Try them out in different orders. Add some. Take some away (and have a discard pile for those, because you might want some back). When you have a particularly successful chain of Cause-and-Effect, photograph it or write it down in your notebook or type it up on your laptop.

You can use cards to plot out your entire play, or just a part of your play that needs work: a passage, sequence, or subplot. You can use them whenever you run into problems in your plot outline regarding what happens when, or what causes what.

Cards make it easier and provide a map

It makes the job easier and more efficient if, instead of pushing around the muddy masses of verbiage described in the Introduction, you're just manipulating a few pieces of cardboard with a few words on them. Then, with your cards in order, you can write some dialogue for them—which will often tell you that the cards are in the wrong order—so then you go back and rearrange the cards—and you continue that way, back and forth. This approach is preferable to negotiating dialogue and plot at the same time. Each side of your brain will be happier doing its own job.

The cards can also form a kind of map of the structure of the play or of a passage. These pictures may show how the cards for some of William's plays might look, laid out this way, although they omit the words on the cards and involve fewer cards than the plays would require. Here's what the cards might look like for *Macbeth*:

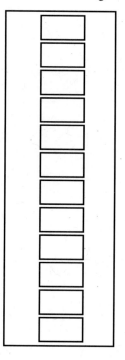

Yes, pretty straightforward. *Macbeth* is William's briefest play, and has no subplots, so the cards are just one column, top to bottom. However, let's say there are other plots impinging on the main plot—such as, in *Hamlet*, the Polonius-family subplot. Its relationship to the main plot might look like this oversimplified version:

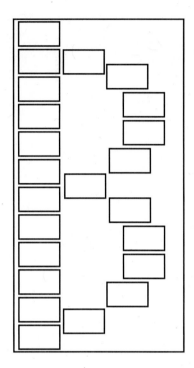

There are two of these "loops" because the subplots impinge on the main plot at three points: when we first meet Polonius and his kids during the opening scenes; when Hamlet kills Polonius around the middle; and when he fights Laertes at the end.

William seems to have liked this structure for his tragedies. It resembles that of *King Lear*, with Gloucester's story looping into Lear's story. (As you've noticed, this version happens to look like a letter B. It doesn't matter on which side of the main plot you place the "loops." A playwriting student with a similar plot structure put one loop on either side, so that the whole thing looked like a dollar sign. She said she was hoping the play would make money.)

William's comedies, on the other hand, tend to be structured with two plots of equal importance running side by side, with occasional connections between them, and with the plots converging at the end when everybody gets married.

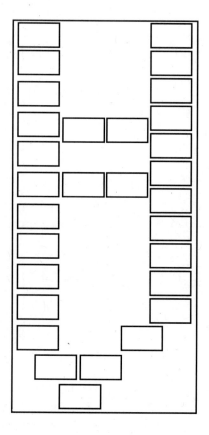

In *A Midsummer-Night's Dream,* the two plots are the shifting affections among the four teenage lovers, and the one-night stand between Bottom and Titania. The connection is Puck, running back and forth with the love potion. Or, if this were a diagram for *Twelfth Night,* the two plots would be the Orsino-Olivia-Viola love triangle and the humiliation of Malvolio. And if it were *The Merry Wives of Windsor,* the two plots would be the Wives setting up assignations between Falstaff and Mistress Ford, and Anne Page being wooed by her three suitors.[38]

Of course, the plays do not feature two scenes playing simultaneously, side by side onstage! The playwright then merges the cards into one column, deciding which plot goes next, scene by scene. You might find

---

38   As mentioned in Chapter 2, William attempted a third plot, but it is incomplete and doesn't work.

it instructive to look at one of these plays of William's and trace which of his plots come back onstage when, and how he arranges them.

Cards show you Cause-and-Effect

The cards help you to see the causes and effects in your play, with each card causing the next. Theoretically, just about any event can be rigged to become the cause or the effect of any other event. When he was a student, actor Ty Olsson was writing a play about an elderly lady—abandoned by her husband, years ago—and her grown children. She's in the habit of buying cheap crockery at flea markets, taking it home, and announcing that it's worth millions of dollars, which it never is. We were helping Ty push his cards around on a table, and he wound up with two "left-over" cards: one said, "VASE WORTH $$$"—i.e., she's finally right, and one of those bits of crockery is indeed worth a fortune—and the other said, "DAD COMES HOME." Ty asked how one of these cards might "cause" the other.

One student suggested that the vase being worth a fortune makes the news, and Dad decides to rejoin his now-wealthy family: thus "VASE WORTH $$$" *caused* "DAD COMES HOME." But another student suggested that in his absence, Dad has become an expert in crockery, and now he walks in the door (for other reasons), sees the vase, and says, "Hey, that thing is worth a million dollars!"—so that "DAD COMES HOME" "caused" "VASE WORTH $$$," or at least caused the family to know it and get rich.

In this case, the vase's great value got rejected, and Dad's homecoming became the main plot. But it's a good example of how *any* two cards can "cause" each other. It's also interesting that the order of those two cards changes Dad's character. If the value of the vase brings him home, he's an opportunist. But if he walks in and generously tells his ex-wife she's a rich woman, then he's a pretty good guy. So in some cases, you may find yourself arranging cards to establish the nature of some of your characters—or changing the character to suit the cards.

The next chapter looks at another play, with which I'm very familiar, and its actual plot cards. They're sitting here on my desk.

6

A Short Play

Totally Nana's Ride

Where this play came from

This play is here to illustrate a few different principles. First of all, it's going to illustrate one way to get started.

In 2015 I was commissioned to write a 10-minute outdoor play, as one of an evening of seven such plays by different playwrights, each one to be performed in or around a parked car. So I started by thinking about moments that I had experienced or heard of, involving cars. I chose two real-life sources, which our list of seven sources in Chapter 2 would categorize as Autobiography and Anecdote.

The Autobiography source: my mother left me her car when she died, and I traded it in a few years later on another. Shortly after that, a cousin was visiting me in Vancouver, we were driving in my newer car around Stanley Park, and I saw my mother's car parked by the side of the road. I pointed it out to my cousin, and had an irrational impulse to pull over, get out and visit it. But since my cousin already considered me a bit of a weirdo, I just kept driving.

The Anecdote source: when my friend Eric and his brother were little boys, they were left alone for a short while in their father's brand-new Jaguar, when he stopped on their way home from the dealership. The boys discovered the cigarette lighter, and decorated Daddy's new car for him, while he was gone, by burning circles into the expensive Corinthian leather seats. (As noted in the script, I got Eric's permission to use this story.)

Some of the subsequent work was done in my head, some was scribbled in a notebook, and some was done using index cards. Here's the play itself, followed by the index cards.

The play itself

Totally Nana's Ride: A short play
Copyright © 2015 John Lazarus

Production History:
Totally Nana's Ride was first performed on July 27, 2015, outdoors at Market Square, Kingston, Ontario, as one of seven ten-minute plays comprising Convergence Theatre's AutoShow, part of the inaugural "Kick and Push Festival" of summer theatre.

Totally Nana's Ride was directed by Rebecca Benson, with automobile procurement and set decoration by Bill Penner, and cars loaned by Travis Cellini and Rod McDonald from Doron Motors. Stage manager was Kristen Leboeuf. The cast was as follows:

ALEX	Zachary Arndt
BRITTANY	Audrey Sturino
JUSTINE	Zahshanné Malik

Acknowledgements:
My thanks to the Kingston writers' group The Inkstons (Ian Coutts, Patty Henderson, Catherine Lyons-King, Cameron Smith, Morgan Wade and Corina Zechel), for dramaturgical advice; and to Eric Depoe, for permission to adapt and use his true story about the cigarette lighter.

Characters: (all three in their 20s)

BRITTANY
ALEX
JUSTINE

The Car:

A 1960s or 1970s Detroit muscle car. In the first production we used a 1963 Dodge Polara and, for some performances, a 1963 Chrysler convertible. The car is messy inside, with blankets, old clothes, newspapers, magazines, food wrappers, empty bottles and cans, and a used condom on the back seat; the front passenger seat is completely covered with garbage. The Car is also grubby on the outside, with the words "I WISH MY G.F. WAS THIS DIRTY" written into the dust.

(ALEX and BRITTANY come down the street.)

ALEX: Trust and commitment! That's what we're celebrating! They go together! We've made a commitment, and now we trust each other to stay committed.

BRITTANY: Right, well, that just seems a little strange coming from you, Allie.

ALEX: Why?

BRITTANY: You know. Mandy?

ALEX: Mandy was three weeks after you and me started dating! That was almost six months ago! We hadn't *made* a commitment yet!

BRITTANY: Well, I thought *I* had. *(Sees Car, stops. ALEX keeps walking. BRITTANY stands still, looking at Car.)*

ALEX: Well, the point is, we have a commitment now, both of us, which is why tonight is such a meaningful—*(Sees that she's fallen behind.)* Hello? Brittany?

BRITTANY: Sorry. This car. This is my grandmother's car.

ALEX: *(Looking around.)* What, I'm gonna meet your grandmother now?

BRITTANY: No, I don't mean this is *actually her car.* I mean it's *identical. (Checks it.)* Yeah. Nineteen sixty-three Dodge

Polara *[or whatever]*. Same make, same model, same year, same colour—under the grime—This is totally Nana's ride!

ALEX: I didn't know you were into cars.

BRITTANY: I'm into *this* car. Or, *her* copy. She called it Simone. Every Friday, Nana and Gramps would pick me up and take me for the weekend. I never knew where we were gonna go. But it was always cool. She was like the coolest person I knew. Maybe ever. When I was older, she told me she and Gramps used to have sex in the back seat of that car.

ALEX: Yeah, that's adorable, thanks for sharing that creepy memory of your grandfather's car, let's go.

BRITTANY: It wasn't my *grandfather's* car. It was *Nana's ride*. Gramps didn't drive. She did the driving, and she scheduled the weekend, and I sat up front with her, and Gramps sat in the back, and we women did the talking. She called us "We women." 'Course, Nana wouldn't let it get like *this*. Eww, there's a used condom on the back seat.

ALEX: Jeez, you think it's your grandparents'?

BRITTANY: That's not funny. It's a different car, they're dead, and when they were alive, they were Catholic. Oh my God, look, somebody even wrote "I wish my girlfriend was this dirty" in the dust on it.

ALEX: *(Sees the writing.)* Oh my God. Oh, jeez. *(Looks around.)*

BRITTANY: What?

ALEX: Uh, nothing, just—that's terrible. That somebody would write that. That they'd let it get so dirty somebody *could* write that. C'mon, we'll be late for the movie.

BRITTANY: No we won't, I just want to stand here beside Nana's ride a minute.

ALEX: Okay this is not Nana's ride, okay? Nana's ride got crushed into a bale, it's in a scrapyard somewhere. Let's go.

BRITTANY: Yeah, but—this is weird, but it doesn't just seem *identical*. It really feels like it's the *same car*. Even with the dirt.

ALEX: Well, we'll never know, will we. So why don't we / just head along to the—

BRITTANY: There'd be one way we could find out. If it had cigarette-lighter burns on the passenger seat. Which we can't see 'cause the seat's covered with crap. But this is a story. One time when I was eight, they both went into a store, and I stayed / in the car—

ALEX: Okay can you tell me on the way to the movie?

BRITTANY: Allie, I don't *care* if we're late for the movie. So I get into the driver's seat and I shove in the cigarette lighter and it pops out and I pretend to smoke. And then, just to see, I press the lighter down on the passenger seat, and it leaves this beautiful black perfect circle. So I make this beautiful pattern of black circles all over the seat: special surprise for my Nana. Are you listening? You keep looking around.

ALEX: I'm riveted.

BRITTANY: When they come back, I show off my work: "Look! Cheerios!" Gramps has a fit. He's like, I am gonna pay to re-upholster that seat, if it means I'm in debt for life. But then Nana says no, she's gonna keep it like it is. As a lesson in not getting attached to material goods. And then she says, to me, it's also a lesson in not messing with other people's stuff. And she never re-did that seat. And I learned not to—*(Sees him.)* Okay, end of story, let's go.

ALEX: Yeah, let's. *(He starts to go. She yanks on the car's door handles, which are locked. ALEX turns, sees.)* Brittany! What'd Nana just say about messing with other people's stuff!

BRITTANY: She also said sometimes you gotta break the rules. *(Pulls on the last of the handles, on the passenger-side front door; it opens.)* Alex! *(She leans into the car, shoves the junk off the passenger seat out onto the ground, and reveals a pattern of black circles on the seat.)* Oh my God. Oh my God. Oh my God. It's Nana's ride. This is actually Nana's actual real car. Simone! You've come back to me! *(Half-lies on the roof, her arms spread across the roof as if to hug the Car.)*

JUSTINE: *(Coming down the street.)* Hey! Excuse me, would you mind not humping my car? *(ALEX hides in the audience. JUSTINE sees her stuff on the ground.)* Whoa! What the hell! What the hell, bitch! You broke into my car!

BRITTANY: It was unlocked.

JUSTINE: *(Takes out her phone.)* It's B and E, unlocked or not! I'm calling the cops! You are so busted! I got witnesses! *(To audience:)* Did any of you guys see—*(Sees ALEX.)* Whoa! Zander! Dude! You never called me after the Alibi! *(Crosses to him, hugs him.)*

ALEX: Uh, yeah, no, sorry.

BRITTANY: "Zander"?

JUSTINE: You were gonna call! It was a week ago tonight! And it was such a great night! And why weren't you at improv yesterday?

BRITTANY: Allie, who is this?

JUSTINE: "Allie"? Oh my God, is this your sister?

ALEX: Brittany, this is Justine. She's in my improv group. Justine, this is Brittany, my girlfriend. Brittany and I are celebrating our six-month anniversary tonight.

JUSTINE: *(Beat.)* Oh my God, you're *Brittany! Wow!* Oh, it is so great to *meet* you! *(Shakes her hand.)* Zander and I are both in this improv class? And so we had a beer a week ago. That's the Alibi. The bar.[39]

BRITTANY: *(To ALEX.)* Was that the night I was in Toronto?

---

39 The Alibi is the name of a real bar in downtown Kingston.

JUSTINE: Yes! And I went down to the Alibi for a drink, and there was Zander, and we started talking, but all he wanted to talk about was *you*, Briony—

BRITTANY: Brittany—

JUSTINE: Brittany, and how much he missed you. Totally adorable.

BRITTANY: I was only gone overnight.

JUSTINE: Yes! And that's why it was totally adorable. And the reason it was a great night is 'cause it showed me how much a guy can care about his woman. And that's why I wanted him to call. To tell me when you got back, so I could meet you. Anyway, it's nice to meet you now.

BRITTANY: Uh, yeah, you too.

JUSTINE: Except why'd you open my car and dump my stuff on the ground? *(ALEX gets busy putting the stuff back in the Car.)*

BRITTANY: Right, sorry. I was trying to see if the burn marks were on the front seat. I made those burn marks. When I was eight. This was my grandmother's car.

JUSTINE: Wow. Really? That is so cool.

BRITTANY: I know, eh?

JUSTINE: Actually, those burn marks are a problem, 'cause I want to sell it.

BRITTANY: You want to *sell* it?

JUSTINE: Yeah, it's kind of a gas guzzler, and it costs a lot in maintenance. But nobody's gonna want it with the burn marks, and I can't afford to replace the seat.

BRITTANY: What're you asking for it?

JUSTINE: Uh, well, I paid five thousand. I would want four.

BRITTANY: I can't afford four. I can give you three thousand, I'll take it as is, and I promise I'll give it a good home.

JUSTINE: Oh. No, sorry. It's a classic, you know. A sixty-three Dodge Polara *[or whatever]*.

BRITTANY: I *know* what it *is*. You just said it was a gas guzzler! High maintenance!

JUSTINE: Nope. Sorry. I'd sell it for four.

BRITTANY: Alex, loan me a thousand bucks!

ALEX: I don't have a thousand bucks.

BRITTANY: *(To JUSTINE.)* I want my Nana's car back! Don't you see what it means to me? It doesn't mean crap to you! Look how you treat it! Somebody wrote "I wish my girlfriend was this dirty" on it! And there's a condom on the back seat! And burn marks on the *front* seat! And you even left it unlocked!

JUSTINE: Yeah, any crazy bitch could get in there. Look, whatever it means to you, Ramone belongs to me, okay?

BRITTANY: "*Ramone*"?

JUSTINE: Guy who sold it to me said it was named it after the Ramones, or the car in the Pixar movie or something.

BRITTANY: It's "Simone"! For Simone de Beauvoir! You can't call it "Ramone"!

JUSTINE: It's my car and I can call it whatever I want. Jeez, "Allie," this is your idea of a girlfriend?

BRITTANY: *I'm gonna kill you! Gimme back my car!*

(She tries to attack JUSTINE, but ALEX holds her back. All three are shouting simultaneously:)

{BRITTANY: I want my grandmother's car back! You have no right to treat it like that!

{ALEX: Brittany, stop it, it's her car, she doesn't gotta sell it if she doesn't want to!

{JUSTINE: You are just one crazy bitch! Control yourself, for God's sake! Christ, no wonder Zander *screws around behind your back!*

BRITTANY: *(Stops.)* What?

ALEX: Aw, Justine…

JUSTINE: I lied just now. What really happened last week, we had a beer at the Alibi and then drove out to Lemoine Point and screwed our brains out in the back seat of the car.

ALEX: Aw, Justine, you were doing so good up to now.

BRITTANY: Allie! That's the back seat my *grandparents* had sex in!

ALEX: Well, I didn't know that!

JUSTINE: Also he's the one who wrote "I wish my girlfriend was this dirty" on it.

BRITTANY: *Allie!*

ALEX: Well, nobody knows it's about *you.*

BRITTANY: I'm not *dirty* enough for you?

JUSTINE: I should add, he wrote that *after* we did it. So it's not even entirely about the car.

BRITTANY: *(To JUSTINE.)* I'm gonna kill you twice. *(May chase her around the car.)*

JUSTINE: Hey, I didn't know he *had* a girlfriend. I don't *do* other women's boyfriends.

BRITTANY: He *wrote it on the car!*

JUSTINE: I thought it was a joke! You know, a thing!

BRITTANY: A thing.

JUSTINE: The truth is, he didn't even mention you. I'm sorry I lied just now about how he missed you. That, I got no excuse. It wasn't even a moral choice or trying to help him out or anything. I just really like improv.

BRITTANY: *(To ALEX.)* "Trust"? "Commitment"?

ALEX: Yeah, sorry.

(Silence.)

BRITTANY: Tell you what. Three thousand and I'll throw in Alex.

ALEX: }
JUSTINE: } What?

BRITTANY: *(Takes out chequebook, writes cheque.)* He's all yours. I renounce all claim to him. We'll do the paperwork on the car tomorrow. Tonight, you go home with Alex and a cheque for three thousand bucks, and I drive off in Simone.

JUSTINE: How do I know he won't screw around on me too?

BRITTANY: You don't. I take Simone as is, you take Alex as is. Look, he may be dumb as a post and a lying cheating hypocritical jackass, / but you got to—

ALEX: Hey, I'm standing right here, / you know—

BRITTANY: You got to admit he's a really good lay. *(To ALEX:)* Something?

ALEX: No.

JUSTINE: Sorry, but isn't there something sort of creepy about this? Like, morally?

BRITTANY: Wow, listen to you. And here I thought you really liked improv.

(Pause.)

JUSTINE: Sold. *(They shake on it.)*

ALEX: Don't I have a say in the deal?

BRITTANY: What would you like to say, Alex?

ALEX: Uhhh…

JUSTINE: *(to BRITTANY.)* Pleasure doing business.

BRITTANY: So. Here's the cheque *(Gives cheque.)*—and here's your signing bonus—*(Re: ALEX.)*

JUSTINE: And here's the keys. *(Hands them over.)*

BRITTANY: Anything special I should know about the car?

JUSTINE: Nah, engine runs good. Anything about Alex?

BRITTANY: Nah, engine runs good. Do you want any of your stuff outa here?

JUSTINE: Are you kidding? The best part of the deal is, I don't have to clean it.

ALEX: That's the best part of the deal?

BRITTANY: Phone me tomorrow. Alex'll give you my number. *(About to go.)*

ALEX: Wait. Brittany. Don't we even get to, like, you know, break up?

BRITTANY: Oh, sure. *(Slaps his face.)* Bye. *(Gets in the Car. If possible, she turns on the radio to the Beach Boys, "Little Old Lady from Pasadena," and drives off.)*

JUSTINE: Cool. C'mon back to my place, let's get some mileage outa you.

ALEX: Wait a second. Wait a second! We didn't use a condom!

JUSTINE: Wow, the penny finally drops, eh?

ALEX: And there was no condom there when we, uh—

JUSTINE: Look, you wanna get laid tonight or not? Let's go. *(Walks away. He follows her. As they go:)*

ALEX: I demand to know where that condom came from!

JUSTINE: Zander, I just acquired you as part of the price for my really old car. Knowing about that condom is above your pay grade.

ALEX: *(Following her off.)* We need to talk about our relationship!

THE END

The cards for Totally Nana's Ride

This section may call for a different kind of reading. As you go through the cards, you may want to flip back to the play itself to remind yourself of how they were translated into dialogue. You may also like to look through the big cards first, to see how the project began, and then look at the small cards to see how it later progressed.

The larger lettering on some of the cards indicates that those are the **big cards**, and the smaller lettering on the others identifies them as the **small cards**. We're using these two different font sizes to make the distinction clear between the two "sizes" of cards. Of course, the physical cards are all the same size!—and on real cards, the letters are usually the same size too. The reference here is to the amount of text, or to the importance of the passage, that each card represents.

As you begin laying out your own plot, you'll probably start with a few big cards, and then, as you progress, interpose among them some newer, smaller cards: more detailed, specialized and numerous. It feels a bit like spreading your fingers on an Internet map to zero in on more detail, or like the "Snowflake Method" mentioned earlier.

Each of the *small* cards below represents the smallest chunk of text that can usefully be moved around. This is called a unit of action, or simply a **unit**:[40] a section of plot outline so detailed that if you got any *more* detailed, you'd actually be writing the dialogue. A unit begins when a character changes objectives, and ends when a character—the same, or another—changes objectives. An **objective** is simply the thing the character wants at a given moment. Some people call them "goals" or "intentions." Entering and exiting count as objectives.

So a unit can be as brief as a gunshot, or, theoretically, as long as the entire play—though in practice, a play consisting of one long unit would be one boring play. However, in practice a unit *can* go on for quite a while and still keep our attention.

Another useful aspect of units is the fact that people can disagree on where one ends and the next one begins. Problems in rehearsal can sometimes be traced to disagreements on where the units change within a sequence.

Cards and dialogue are a two-way, mutual process: writing the dialogue gives you information that feeds back into the cards. For example, the layout below includes two that got discarded, after the dialogue was written, and there are also cards that the characters created in the course of my writing the dialogue. (Yes, "that the characters created": it is useful to imagine that the characters themselves are coming up with this stuff.)

AL is Alex, BR is Brittany, NA is Nana, GR is Gramps (though these two don't appear in the play), and JUS is Justine.

---

40 Some people, like Greenblatt in his *Text and Context*, use the term "beat" to mean what I mean by "unit." I use the word "beat" to mean a very short pause, which takes up one beat in the rhythm of the dialogue. There's one in *Totally Nana's Ride*: Justine takes a "beat" just after Alex introduces her to Brittany, while she decides to help him with his deception.

Sometimes a unit reveals or establishes a fact known to the characters but not to the audience. I write "ESTAB:" on cards that describe those establishings.

Brittany seeing the car marks the first interruption in the routine, which was to walk to the movie theatre. It is the introduction of what will become the conflict.

ESTAB:
CAR IS IDENTICAL
TO NANA'S

BR STARTS CAR STORY:
WEEKEND DRIVES

BR CAR STORY CONT'D:
NA & GR HAD SEX
IN BACK SEAT

AL & BR SEE USED CONDOM

Originally, it was the used condom that told Alex this was the car he'd been in with Justine. But then I found a picture on the Internet of a truck with "I WISH MY WIFE WAS THIS DIRTY" written in the grime, so I stole that idea. But I kept the used condom in the back seat, hoping it might pay off another way, as indeed it does at the end of the play.

As always, the audience's antennae are out, so they believe that Brittany, who assumes this is a normal date in real life, won't notice his desperation to get her away from that car, while the audience, knowing it's a play, notices it very well. They may not know yet why he's afraid, but they can probably guess.

Alex trying to move Brittany along to the movie is presented here as a separate unit from her telling the story, though the two actions later got intermingled in the dialogue. Yes, you can do that.

The original big card, above, later sprouted a small card before it and one after it, because it's generally best to keep each unit on its own card. You never know if two or more units might wind up in different parts of the play; keeping them on one card may prevent you from seeing those possibilities. In this case, the cards remained together through the process, which of course is not a problem.

BR REMOVES GARBAGE,
SEES BURN MARKS

BR CELEBRATES,
CLIMBS ONTO HOOD

JUS FINDS BR
SNOOPING IN CAR

JUS ENTERS,
SEES BR ON HOOD

AL HIDES IN AUDIENCE

JUS SEES THAT
BR OPENED CAR

JUS THREATENS COPS,
ASKS AUDIENCE FOR WITNESSES

JUS SEES AL IN AUDIENCE

She's motivated to look into the audience (which, for this show, was a group of people standing around on the sidewalk), to ask for witnesses. This is cooler—that is, more motivated—than if she'd just happened to glance into the audience and see him.

JUS HUGS AL, SAYS
"WHY DIDN'T YOU CALL?" ETC.

AL INTRODUCES JUS TO BR,
BEGS HER NOT TO BLOW HIS COVER

Yes, he does indeed beg her, in the subtext! "This is Brittany, my girlfriend. Brittany and I are celebrating our six-month anniversary tonight" is a loud, though disguised, cry for help.

JUS PLAYS ALONG,
INVENTS COVER STORY

The *playwright's* reason for Justine to play along, rather than blowing Alex's cover immediately, is to give her and Brittany time to talk about the car and discuss its possible sale before Brittany learns of the affair. The *character's* reason—Justine's motivation—is that, as she later explains, "I just really like improv." And this provided the idea that they'd met at an improv class.

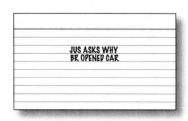

JUS ASKS WHY
BR OPENED CAR

Again, two cards for two moments that obviously go together—but might not have.

And yet again, I originally put these two moments on two different cards, in case for some reason I might later want to separate them. And yet again, as we now know, I didn't.

Verbs like "negotiate," "talk about," "discuss," "converse," etc., can be red flags in cards and plot outlines, suggesting inactive sequences. But in this case, that's what they have to do. And the negotiation increases their mutual annoyance, which in turn motivates Justine to blurt out the truth.

Admittedly, that's a weird card. But they do have to calm down for a moment so that they can get to Brittany's offer.

Let's digress briefly to a moral and political question that rose here, as a character offers to trade another human being to a third character. Just how offensive this is depends on the characters' genders. I tried every possible combination of genders and orientations—knowing full well that changing even one would have meant rewriting the whole play, but that's show biz. But I concluded that the only acceptable one was the one I'd started with: two women trading a man. And after all, Alex is not literally being bought and sold. He's merely getting a new, less gullible, less faithful girlfriend.

This is one of the two discarded cards, which is why it's crossed out. Brittany explained to Justine why Alex wouldn't sneak back to Brittany. But the more she explained, the more this looked like a plot point that would pay off later, which it isn't. Besides, the play had to time out at exactly 10 minutes, and this was taking too long.

It was an interesting reversal to let Brittany be, for a moment, bolder and more outrageous than Justine. It's nice when a character surprises you.

Justine's "Sold" is the climax of the play, the resolution of the conflict, so that's the last big card. The rest is dénouement, so it's all small cards.

Necessary business, but with opportunities for comedy.

Another discard: to seal the deal, the two women shared a hug, and Alex tried to join in, but was pushed away. On paper it seemed funny, but in rehearsal it just felt sour. Sometimes you can't tell until it's on its feet.

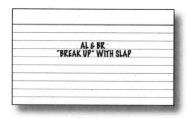

This moment went the other way: on paper it had seemed hurtful, but it was usually greeted with a guffaw from the audience.

In performance, the actor was not allowed to drive the borrowed car, so she sat in the driver's seat while Alex and Justine finished the show.

And here, the condom pays off after all, by showing Alex that he now has a girlfriend who will cheat on him like he cheated on Brittany, but who, unlike Alex with Brittany, doesn't care if he knows it.

7

Dialogue, Part 1

What Dialogue Says

We're not all born knowing how to write dialogue

This chapter introduces the dialogue-writing Way About It. It seems most playwrights, including myself, write dialogue comparatively easily, and must study how to write plot. But a sizeable minority are comfortable constructing plot, and must study writing dialogue. For them, and for the natural dialogue-writers who want to be sure they're on the right track, here's how dialogue is written.

Start with two characters. In writing a scene of three or more characters, you must continually decide not only what is said next but also who says it, so, assuming you're new to this, let's start with two.

At least one needs an objective. There's nothing wrong with giving them both objectives: when Hamlet enters Gertrude's room, her objective is to call him out for offending Claudius, and his is to rebuke her for marrying Claudius in the first place (and Polonius' is to eavesdrop and find out what's going on). In any case, start by imagining you're the character with an objective. To pursue "your" objective with the other character, you have an impulse to say something. What do you want to say to that person? Write that down.

Now switch over, and "be" the second character, and read the line you just wrote, imagining it's being said to you. "You," the character, may not have had an objective before, but now this first character has said something which forces you to respond, and your new objective is in your response. What do you want to say in reply to what this other character just said? Write that down. Now switch back to the first character—and on you go.

As an example of how this works, let's go back to the opening of *Totally Nana's Ride*. Here, again, is the first unit: six lines, establishing the routine before it is interrupted by Brittany's seeing the Car.

> ALEX: Trust and commitment! That's what we're celebrating! They go together! We've made a commitment, and now we trust each other to stay committed.

> BRITTANY: Right, well, that just seems a little strange coming from you, Allie.

> ALEX: Why?

> BRITTANY: You know. Mandy?

> ALEX: Mandy was three weeks after you and me started dating! That was almost six months ago! We hadn't *made* a commitment yet!

> BRITTANY: Well, I thought *I* had. *(Sees Car, stops.)*

The play begins with the two of them *in medias res*, as they say, which is "into the middle of things" in Latin. Alex's opening line, "Trust and commitment!" etc., sounds like they've already been talking. If you want to begin your play in mid-conversation like this, think about the offstage or pre-show conversation that's led to it. In our production, the actors entered[41] the street from a restaurant, so I imagined that as they'd been heading for the restaurant door, Alex had said something like, "I think what we're

---

41 Yes, "entered"—even though they came out of a building to the outdoors. In the theatre, "enter" means to come into the audience's view, and "exit" means to leave the audience's view. So they didn't "exit" the restaurant; they "entered from" it.

really celebrating tonight is our trust and commitment," and Brittany had said something like, "What are you talking about?" and had headed out into the street. So Alex's first line is his answer to her question.

Then, "as" Brittany, I read the line as if addressed to me—"and now we trust each other to stay committed"—and, remembering the Mandy affair, I thought, "Heck of a thing for him to say," so I "said," as Brittany (in reality, writing it down, of course), "Right, well, that just seems a little strange coming from you, Allie." Then I pretended to be Alex again, and read that line as if it had been said to me, and wrote, "Why?"

The playwright's reason for the "Why?" was simply to keep the dialogue going. As the playwright, you should also imagine your own "character's reason," but be prepared to hear the actor or director find a different one. The actor might play "Why?" to indicate that he'd forgotten all about Mandy, or that he knows what Brittany means and resents having to deal with it, or that he knows but is pretending he forgot. He might even try it differently in different performances. I don't know what motivation actor Zachary Arndt chose for that moment. It worked—meaning it was both interesting and believable—and that was all I cared about.

So now I'm Brittany again, and he's asked why I thought "trust and commitment" were strange things for him to brag about, so I remind him of Mandy. And now I'm Alex, and she's brought up Mandy, so I leap to my defence: "Mandy was three weeks after you and me started dating! That was almost six months ago! We hadn't *made* a commitment yet!" And as Brittany, I'm a little hurt by this, because I remember thinking we had something special, even that early, so I say, "Well, I thought *I* had"—and then I see the car.

Of course, the improvising of dialogue in the playwright's mind usually happens faster than this written version may imply; it can ripple along very rapidly. And by the way, what you, as the playwright, do in improvising the dialogue is similar to what your actors will do in rehearsal. Just as you explore the impulses that lead your characters to say these lines, the cast will explore them again later, in effect reverse-engineering them and trying to reproduce your thinking.

Sometimes, while writing dialogue, it helps to keep half an eye on its expository purpose, but sometimes it's better to forget, if you can, that "you" are in a play with a plot, and to think like the characters in their delusion that this is real life. If as a result your characters depart from your plot outline, you can deal with that later, as described further along in this chapter. "Forgetting" the plot can help prevent you from trying to use both sides of your brain at once, and it keeps your dialogue from becoming **expository**.

The art of exposition

In Chapter 1, introducing the idea of motivation as the character's reason which disguises the storyteller's reason, "expository" dialogue was cited as a common example of unmotivated action. "Expository" (noun form, "exposition") is one of those words with two meanings: a neutral one and a pejorative one.[42] The neutral meaning of "expository" is "meant to explain something" to the audience or reader. Essays and lectures are unashamedly expository. This book is expository. But the pejorative meaning kicks in when the playwright's reason is, yes, to explain something to the audience, but the character's reason doesn't properly hide it, so the exposition is unmotivated.[43]

Expository dialogue often takes the form of characters telling each other things they both already know, so that the audience gets the information spoon-fed to them. This kind of dialogue crops up even in the classics. The opening scene in Henrik Ibsen's *Hedda Gabler* consists of two characters sharing info already known to both. Juliane, whose nephew Jörgen has just married the title character Hedda, is chatting with her former maid, Berthe. They remind each other that the honeymooners' boat got in late last

---

42 For another example, "amateur" is neutral when describing an actual amateur but insulting when describing someone who claims to be a professional.

43 Mike Myers gets deliberately expository in his parodistic *Austin Powers* movies, with the character Basil Exposition (Michael York) explaining to Powers and the audience what his mission and weapons are going to be in the movie. This is Meyers taking the usually disguised task of exposition and bringing it to the surface as a joke.

night; that Berte will now work for Hedda; that Juliane's sister, Jörgen's mother, is now very ill; and so on.

Even William sometimes falls into that trap. In *The Tempest*, Prospero, a powerful wizard, commands two slaves: Ariel, a spirit of air, and the semi-human, "savage and deformed" Caliban. Early in the play,[44] Prospero reminds Ariel, in detail, that Caliban's mother, the witch Sycorax, imprisoned Ariel in a tree for years, until Prospero freed him, et cetera. And a few minutes later, Prospero informs Caliban that Caliban tried to rape Prospero's young daughter Miranda, and Caliban informs Prospero that Prospero prevented him.

And in fairness to these masters, it should be said that for unmotivated and obvious exposition, neither of these two plays surpasses *The Late Blumer* (1984) by John Lazarus, which opens with an indigestible chunk of backstory, told by a character to another character who has heard it before.

But don't let these cautionary examples discourage you. Often this problem has a simple solution: introduce another character who doesn't know what's going on, so that those characters can inform the uninformed character, and thus the audience. In fact, in that same early scene in *The Tempest*, William uses for this purpose Prospero's daughter Miranda, to whom the old man reveals his own life story—motivated by the fact that his enemies have just now been marooned on his island, thanks to the tempest of the title, which he himself has magically whipped up, and he has to get her ready to meet them.

My first inkling of this technique came when I was 16, playing Colonel Pickering in a teenage production of *My Fair Lady*, the 1954 musical by Alan Jay Lerner and Frederick Loewe, based on George Bernard Shaw's 1913 play *Pygmalion*, about a linguistics professor named Henry Higgins who teaches an impoverished young Cockney woman named Eliza Doolittle to speak like an aristocratic English lady, and so transforms both their lives. My character, Pickering, is Higgins' friend.

---

44 Act 1, Sc. 2.

While learning my lines for the opening scene, in which the three characters first meet, I suddenly caught a glimpse of the mechanics of motivation: exploiting the characters' conversation to tell the audience stuff. Higgins has been impressing the crowd outside the Royal Opera House at Covent Garden by deducing their various origins from their accents. Now the crowd has dispersed, and the three of them are alone on the sidewalk. This is the original Shaw, though slightly abridged and without his eccentric punctuation, formatting, and character names:

PICKERING: How do you do it, if I may ask?

HIGGINS: Simply phonetics. The science of speech. That's my profession: also my hobby. Happy is the man who can make a living by his hobby! *You* can spot an Irishman or a Yorkshireman by his brogue. *I* can place any man within six miles. I can place him within two miles in London. Sometimes within two streets. [...]

PICKERING: But is there a living in that?

HIGGINS: Oh yes. Quite a fat one. This is an age of upstarts. Men begin in Kentish Town with eighty pounds a year, and end in Park Lane with a hundred thousand. They want to drop Kentish Town; but they give themselves away every time they open their mouths. [...] You see this creature with her kerbstone English: the English that will keep her in the gutter to the end of her days. Well, sir, in three months I could pass that girl off as a duchess at an ambassador's garden party. I could even get her a place as lady's maid or shop assistant, which requires better English. That's the sort of thing I do for commercial millionaires. And on the profits of it I do genuine scientific work in phonetics, and a little as a poet on Miltonic lines.

PICKERING: I am myself a student of Indian dialects; and—

HIGGINS: *(Eagerly.)* Are you? Do you know Colonel Pickering, the author of Spoken Sanscrit?

PICKERING: I am Colonel Pickering. Who are you?

HIGGINS: Henry Higgins, author of Higgins' Universal Alphabet.

PICKERING: *(With enthusiasm.)* I came from India to meet you.

HIGGINS: I was going to India to meet you.

PICKERING: Where do you live?

HIGGINS: Twenty-seven-A Wimpole Street. Come and see me tomorrow.

PICKERING: I'm at the Carlton. Come with me now and let's have a jaw over some supper.

HIGGINS: Right you are.

With this dialogue, Shaw both lays out the theme of the play and kick-starts the plot into gear, for Eliza, who is no dolt, overhears and memorize the address, and shows up the next day to challenge him to teach her to speak like a lady. And yet it's all covered up and disguised by Higgins' motivations—which are, in the manner of professors everywhere, to share his enthusiasm for his subject, and also to impress this intelligent and curious gentleman with his expertise. Motivated exposition.

But another way to deal with exposition is by not providing it!—or at least not until later. The playwright's job is opposite to the journalist's. In journalism, it's unprofessional to "bury the lede"[45]—to take the central facts, which should appear in the opening sentences, and conceal them until later in the story. On the contrary, it is often the playwright's *job* to bury the lede.

When Jerry opens Edward Albee's 1958 one-act *The Zoo Story* by announcing to a stranger, "I've been to the zoo," the audience doesn't know why he starts the conversation until the end of the play. Most crime mysteries depend on our not knowing the central facts. *Oedipus Rex* is a different play to those who know in advance

---

45   As you've no doubt guessed, "lede" means the "lead item," the most important part of the story, but it's spelled "lede" so as not to confuse it with the strip of "lead" metal, pronounced "led," that separates the lines of type.

why there's a plague upon Thebes, and those who do not. And if you didn't know *Macbeth*, it would be a nice kick at the end when Macduff reveals why Macbeth will not be safe from Macduff's sword.

Making the audience wait for the information is an actor's and director's trick too. At the climax of William's *Measure for Measure*, the heroine, Isabella, must decide whether to spare the life of the man who she thinks killed her brother. At a 1969 rehearsal at the Stratford Festival, in which the late, great actor William Hutt directed that scene, the actor playing Isabella wasn't taking enough time over the decision for Hutt's taste, so he exclaimed, "Make them wait! That's what they've paid for!" Good advice to playwrights too.

When characters go rogue

> The trick is to stand not knowing certain things long enough for them to come to you.
>
> —Lynda Barry [46]

If, as is recommended earlier in this chapter, you try to think like the characters and forget that there's a play while you're writing their dialogue, then your characters may go off on tangents and refuse to stick to your plot outline. Why, it's almost as though they didn't know there was one! Two characters whom you need to be enemies might get along just fine, or two who were supposed to form a firm friendship might be at each other's throats.

This wandering of your characters away from your plot outline is part of the process, and, although you need to fix it, you haven't screwed up. In fact, it's a good sign: it means that they're thinking for themselves, so to speak, and becoming three-dimensional. But now they've given you a choice to make.

You can decide that what they're doing is more interesting than your original plot outline and rewrite your outline and/or cards to follow these new developments. Or, if you still think your original plot idea is more engaging than what the characters are doing, you

---

46 *Picture: This* (Montreal: Drawn and Quarterly, 2010), 117.

can rewrite their dialogue to steer them back to your plot outline. That kind of decision-making recurs throughout the writing.

I discovered the Two Ways About It approach as a way to maintain control of the material, but *maintaining* is just one Way About It. There's also much to be said for deliberately *losing* control sometimes: putting your plot aside for a while, and following your characters on their own byways, to see if they take you somewhere new. This can be productive when you're confident that you can find your way back or change the route. And sometimes it can give you that lovely feeling that many creative artists speak of: that sense that you're just a medium through which the inspiration flows.

Active dialogue

There is an unfortunate idea that live stage plays are inherently boring, because they convey much of the action of the play by means of dialogue. This stereotype may be due to all those chat plays—or perhaps the reason people write all those chat plays is because they think plays should be boring! However, whether their action is conveyed by means of dialogue or not, good plays are *active*.

For one thing, there's plenty of opportunity for physical action onstage. William offers it in many forms: sword fights, battle scenes, shipwrecks, murders and suicides, alarums and excursions, ghostly visitations, magic spells by witches, fairies and wizards, drunken brawls, masked balls, a wrestling match, a queen hauling a servant by his hair, and that unfortunate gentleman who exits, pursued by a bear.

But also, the dialogue in a play can and should be what's called **active dialogue**. The term may seem vague at first, but when you start looking for it in any kind of fiction, the distinction between active and inactive dialogue grows clearer. Examples of active dialogue might include such phrases as, "I want to go to bed with you," "I'm pregnant and it's yours," "Will you marry me?" "I want a divorce," "You have Stage Four cancer," "We find the defendant guilty," "Kill Claudio," "Luke, I am your father"—and even "Three thousand and I'll throw in Alex."

Active dialogue is dialogue that moves the plot forward; that characters speak to pursue their objectives; that makes the audience turn to look at the other characters to see how they're taking it. (Sometimes, outside a theatrical context, and especially in the legal world, these kinds of sentences are called "speech acts"—such as, "I now pronounce you husband and wife.")

A student, writing a play about a gay teenager coming out, said in class, "If he says to his best friend, 'I'm in love with your brother,' would you call that active dialogue?" And one of the other students said, "Yeah, but if he says to the guy, 'I'm in love with *you*,' then that's *really* active dialogue." Quite right.

Of course, not every line moves the plot forward. Lines have many purposes: to give us background information, to set a mood, or merely to make things feel real. But if you can get such lines to serve double duty, and move the story forward at the same time, then you've got something exciting going.

Subtext versus on-the-nose writing

It's been a long-recognized fact that we don't always say what we mean. **Subtext** is, perhaps obviously, the deeper meaning beneath the text. Actors and directors are always dealing with subtext, winkling out what the character really means behind what's being said, and then it becomes part of the fun for the audience too. Planting that subtext and covering it up is the playwright's job.

Sometimes subtext is deliberately intended by the character, to convey not-so-hidden meanings. Hamlet hides his true feelings from everybody except Horatio and the audience, but his lines to other characters often have this kind of subtext. In his very first line, calling Claudius "A little more than kin, and less than kind," the first part is a response to Claudius' just having acknowledged that Hamlet is both his nephew and now his stepson, and the second part is a pun on "kind": that, related or not, they're not the same kind of man, and that Claudius is unkind. A few lines later, when Gertrude joins Claudius in urging Hamlet to stay home and not go back to university in Wittenberg, he says, "I shall in all my best obey you, Madam."[47] How obvious the subtext is in that line often depends on the emphasis the actor places on the word "you."

Another example of subtext as veiled communication comes up in that same first scene in *Hedda Gabler* that we looked at earlier. This example occurs later in the scene, when Jörgen and his Aunt Juliane are chatting. She's asking about the honeymoon and their plans for the future. It is clear to the audience, though not to Jörgen, that she's really asking whether the couple are likely to have a child soon. Clueless Jörgen assumes she's talking about his scholarly work. She mentions an extra room in the house which might be put to good use, meaning as a nursery; he thinks she means he might use it as an office. The audience realizes that Jörgen and Hedda may not even have consummated the marriage. Keeping sexual matters in the subtext was appropriate for a European writer in 1891—Ibsen was criticized for being scandalously frank anyway, even with his carefully veiled dialogue—but keeping this meaning under the surface also adds to both the drama and the comedy of the situation.

There's another kind of subtext, which peeks accidentally through the surface, especially if a character is being deceptive. In William's *Othello*, the villain, Iago, convinces Othello that his wife, Desdemona, is having an affair with another officer, Cassio. (She isn't.) In this passage early in the play, Iago starts out with a bit of a fishing expedition, trying to sound out Cassio about any sexual feelings he might actually have for Desdemona, or at least to get him to say something Iago might use later. Cassio does not rise to the bait. Read for subtext:

CASSIO: Welcome, Iago; we must to the watch.

IAGO: Not this hour, lieutenant; 'tis not yet ten o' the clock. Our general cast us thus early for the love of his Desdemona; who let us not therefore blame: he hath not yet made wanton the night with her; and she is sport for Jove.

CASSIO: She's a most exquisite lady.

IAGO: And, I'll warrant her, full of game.

---

47 Act 1, Sc. 2.

CASSIO: Indeed, she's a most fresh and delicate creature.

IAGO: What an eye she has! Methinks it sounds a parley of provocation.

CASSIO: An inviting eye; and yet methinks right modest.

IAGO: And when she speaks, is it not an alarum to love?

CASSIO: She is indeed perfection.

IAGO: Well, happiness to their sheets![48]

On the surface, this is just two guys chatting about an attractive woman they know. But the passage is full of subtext. Iago suggests that Othello put them on the watch early so that he could grab some alone time with Desdemona. ("Sport for Jove" refers to the Roman god whose idea of sport was sex with beautiful women.) He implies that she flirts with other men: her eye is "a parley of provocation," her voice "an alarum to love." Cassio, however, is loath to say anything improper about his commanding officer's virtuous lady wife, so he deflects Iago's raunchy comments with respectful praise. Clearly, he wishes Iago wouldn't talk like that, but doesn't want to say so. His "She is indeed perfection" seems to say, "Yeah, fine, she's perfect, can we drop this?" And at that, with "Well, happiness to their sheets!" Iago gives up for the moment.

Often, in rehearsal, an actor or director will decide on subtext you didn't intend. Don't assume that's a bad thing or be too quick to jump in and "correct" them: their choice may work better! There's more about this in the chapters on workshops, readings and rehearsals, but for now, let's just say that if your dialogue is consistent in its subtext and motivations, then those that the cast decide on will likely be consistent too, even if they're different from yours.

The opposite to dialogue rich in subtext is called "on-the-nose" dialogue, which explicitly describes the character's emotions of the moment. It's usually expository-sounding, not very interesting, and to be avoided. One way to identify it is as anything that could

---

48   Act 2, Sc. 3.

be preceded with the character saying, "Let's talk about how I'm feeling right now…"

William was sometimes guilty of writing on the nose. For example: Romeo and his buddies have crashed Juliet's parents' masked ball.[49] Juliet's cousin Tybalt recognizes Romeo under his mask and wants to throw him out, but his uncle Capulet forbids him, not wanting to ruin their nice party. Tybalt is left shaking with frustration and tells us so in an aside to the audience: "Patience perforce with wilful choler meeting / Makes my flesh tremble in their different greeting." "Patience perforce" means patience forced on him by Capulet—"wilful choler" is anger full of wilfulness—and that couplet is on-the-nose dialogue.

In this context, playwright and teacher Judith Thompson shared with me a great rule for students: no shrink scenes!—a "shrink" meaning not just a psychiatrist or psychologist, but a member of the clergy, a social worker, a bartender—anybody whose *job* it is to listen to other people's troubles.

It's an excellent rule for several reasons. For one, shrink scenes obliterate subtext. The "patient" character simply explains exactly how they feel right now, in on-the-nose dialogue. For another, the "shrink" character is often not much of a character, but a cardboard figure whose job is merely to listen. And for a third, when the shrink does speak up, it is often to reveal that the playwright doesn't know much about how real shrinks do their work.

In practice, many a shrink scene can be saved, or at least improved, by giving the "shrink" character a name and making him a friend, relative, or other sort of confidant, with problems of his own. That motivates *both* characters to speak *less* directly—which, in the theatre, can be a good thing—and allow for more subtext.

Dialogue for crowds (and three's a crowd)

There's not much to add here about the craft of writing passages with three or more characters. As mentioned above, it becomes part of your job to decide who speaks next. Again, one or more

---

49 Act 1, Sc. 5.

characters may not have an objective in mind at the beginning of the passage, but should develop one pretty soon, based on what the other characters want. You may also have to occasionally "check in" mentally with the characters who are not speaking. But don't worry if a character isn't speaking for a while: sometimes it's the silent character who holds the audience's attention. (The next chapter contains a passage from Erin Shields' *Soliciting Temptation*, which is a good example of this from a two-character play. One character, a young sex worker, doesn't say a word for the first several minutes of the play, while her customer natters on nervously. In performance, the audience becomes fascinated by her.) There's a useful process called the "Solo Workshop," described in Chapter 13, for going back over a passage and making sure that each character's journey is represented.

8

Dialogue, Part 2

How Dialogue Says It

"All my characters sound the same!"

This is one of the commonest complaints among playwrights about their own work. (It's worse when somebody *else* says, "All *your* characters sound the same.") This chapter is intended to help with that. It's about people's unconscious verbal habits, the rhythm of real conversation and written dialogue—and about "chewability" (how the dialogue feels in the actors' mouths) and "inkfish" (excess verbiage that can be removed so that the dialogue fits in those actors' mouths better). You'll also learn a game called "Eavesdropping."

How are people talking now?

Start listening to the stuff we're not "supposed" to listen to—people's unconscious verbal habits—the "ah"s and "um"s and little verbal cues that we make to keep each other talking: "Yeah," "Uh-huh," the famous Canadian "eh," and so on. A colleague calls these "Kay-sos." "'Kay, so I was walking down the street..." If you're writing about contemporary characters, it can be an interesting challenge to try to catch these in people's conversation and import them into your work before they have made it into the dialogue of other writers! It's those small verbal habits that help to make your dialogue sound current, and also to distinguish your different characters.

Rhythm

Determining a rhythm for a specific character can help you make that character's dialogue distinctive. Of course, "rhythm" in dialogue is naturally looser and more relaxed than the constant, recurring beats in music. The best ways to get familiar with rhythm in dialogue are by listening for it in real-life conversation, noting how it occurs in other writers' dialogue, and looking for it in your own work.

As will be explained later in this chapter, part of what you're listening for when you play the Eavesdropping game is the different rhythms in people's conversation. But you can *always* listen for rhythms in the conversations around you. What words are stressed and what words are not? How long or short are people's phrasings? How, and how often, do they inhale while talking?

It can also be instructive to look at rhythms in the work of other writers of fiction, especially fellow playwrights. Of my generation, David Mamet is known for the rhythms of his dialogue, and earlier playwrights such as Harold Pinter, Tennessee Williams, and Arthur Miller were praised for theirs. (Miller had a way of sneaking iambic pentameter into his dialogue: in *The Crucible*, protagonist John Proctor says, "Massachusetts is a glory in the spring.")

Here are two examples of compelling spoken rhythms in contemporary theatre. The first is from *Tombs of the Vanishing Indian* by Métis performer / playwright / director / filmmaker Marie Clements. The character Jessie is described as "an idealist physician who is married to a medical colleague." Note how the repetition adds to the hypnotic effect of the rhythm.

> JESSIE: I dreamed once I had a mother and she had me, and I had two sisters, and she had them, and we were on a bus, with a skinny grey dog on the side, and my younger sister barfed on the floor, and it smelled and my other sister buried her baby face in my mother's deep breast and drank like that river was hers. I dreamed once I had a mother and she had me and I

had two sisters and she had them and we were on a bus with a skinny grey dog on the side, and we were travelling a long way to make a new story, and it was hot and my mother opened the bus window, and a beautiful stream of wind came over us and it blew my mother's black hair all over our round faces that laid on my mother's body like we owned her. She said, just then, "Look girls, look at those rocks." These three big boulders standing just so in the desert, staring just enough for us to recognize them. She said, "Jessie, look, don't you recognize them from home, look how they stand," and I said, "Yes, I think I do." She said, "Jessie, the rock family are following us to L.A, to start a new life too." Such are the things memories are made of.[50]

Here's one more example: a passage from *Soliciting Temptation* by Canadian playwright and teacher Erin Shields. The setting is "a hotel room in a developing country." The character, a white man in his 50s called only "Man," addresses a young, non-white, female sex worker, "Girl," who has come to his room. Note how the stop-start rhythm expresses his nervousness before this very young-looking woman who has not spoken yet. The free-verse formatting is Shields'. The passage begins as the Man has just opened the door to the Girl.

MAN: You're…here.

Beat.

Come in.
Please.
Come in.

She does.

He closes the door.

I'm sorry.
About the smell.
It's me.
Haha.
Haven't had a shower.

---

50 *Refractions: Solo*, ed. Donna-Michelle St. Bernard and Yvette Nolan (Toronto: Playwrights Canada Press, 2014), 4.

That is, I took one this morning but I've only just returned to
find the maid has flipped off the switch for the hot.
Hot water.
Conserving energy, I imagine, saving money.
Not that I need it.
Hot, that is.
Hot enough in here and the air conditioner's on the fritz.
Stopped working sometime in the night.
Woke up in a pool of sweat and thought I'd come down with it.
Malaria or yellow fever or something yet unnamed,
though my shots are up to date
and I'm pretty good with the Malarone,
but I suppose you never know what strain
of delirium the mosquitoes will think of next.
Buzz.

> *Beat.*

I really can't sleep in the net.
Does it ever bother you?

> *Beat.*

I wacked it a few times.
The air conditioner, not the net.
That's what we do,
we men who don't work with our hands,
haha.
It breaks, you kick it, you get on the phone.
Club hands of thumbs, that's what these are.
My wife won't let me anywhere near light bulbs or hammers
and I stub my toe on something different every morning.
How old did you say you were?

> *Beat.*

Never ask a woman her age.
Learned that the hard way.
Haha.[51]

---

51   Erin Shields, *Soliciting Temptation* (Toronto: Playwrights Canada Press,
2015), pp. 5–6.

Another way of getting comfortable with rhythms in dialogue is, of course, to look for it, and develop it, in your own work. This means reading your dialogue out loud. There will be more to say about this in Chapter 13, on Rewriting—and more coming right up:

Chewability and inkfish

An important aspect of dialogue is the actual feel of the words in the actors' lungs and mouths. This is one reason why working as an actor yourself—amateur, student or professional—can be valuable to a playwright. It gives you the experience of breathing out, and wrapping your mouth around, another writer's words. It helps you to understand, as a playwright, how important it is to write dialogue that is "chewable," or, as Hamlet says, spoken "trippingly on the tongue."[52] But, of course, you can do this without becoming an actor—simply while writing your own dialogue. Playwrights are known for mumbling and muttering aloud as we sit at our laptops.

Another thing you're looking for in your own work—in this case, to remove it—is what's called "inkfish," a term I learned from the Los Angeles hip-hop poet and theatre artist reg. e. gaines, when he visited our Playwriting class at Queen's some years ago. It turns out that an inkfish is *not* just a cephalopod mollusk related to the squid! By reg's definition, it's also that extra dollop of ink on the page: the extra verbiage you don't need. Most drafts of most scripts suffer from inkfish. Most can use an obsessive going-over, to wipe up and throw away those extra blobs. reg made the point that bringing inkfish to the attention of a colleague is an act of politeness, like mentioning that someone's fly is open or that they have a drop of sauce on their chin.

I considered placing the discussion of inkfish in Chapter 13, on Rewriting, but I think it belongs here, as another tool for distinguishing your characters and making life easier for your actors. Both to enhance rhythm and to eliminate inkfish— sometimes the same activity—a playwright goes over and over the same passage of dialogue in her mind, rewriting, trimming, trying different words, and "chewing" on it: looking for what works best with the actor's breath and vocal equipment. It's not a complicated

52   Act 3, Sc. 2.

process, or a cerebral one: it's physical and emotional. And this part of the job often distinguishes the accomplished playwright from the beginner.

Try it. Take a passage of a few lines from the play you're writing: a passage you think needs work, or one you're proud of, or one you haven't thought much about either way. Memorize it. Carry it around in your head for a few days. Keep rewriting it in your mind and notice how the different versions feel in your mouth.

Be aware of when, how, and how often you have to breathe, to speak them. Big breaths or small? Several breaths, or does a line work best in one go, without inhaling in the middle? When do you have to swallow? Where do you have four words where one would do? Three of those words are inkfish. And sure, sometimes you can choose to leave the inkfish there—but you can't make that choice if you haven't noticed it's there in the first place. Listen to the vowels and the consonants. Enjoy the rhythm, or improve it. See where you can make it more chewable, or more breathable, or shorter, or just plain better.

Grammars

Of course, many fictional characters speak with technically "incorrect" grammar. It's perfectly acceptable for Arthur Miller to have Eddie, in *A View from the Bridge,* say "Whitey don't sing; he don't do like that on the ships," or for me to have Alex, in *Totally Nana's Ride,* say "after you and me started dating" or "you were doing so good up to now." And there's nothing wrong with Lorraine Hansberry's characters in *A Raisin in the Sun* speaking in an authentic African-American dialect, as you'll read in Chapter 11. But if you're writing in a specific style or dialect, make sure that it's accurate—or, if your play is set in an imaginary world or a country where they're understood to be speaking a different language, at least interesting and believable. And your introductory material, stage directions, and any other writing that is not dialogue, should be consistent.

That said, there's a current movement arguing that traditionally "correct" grammar and spelling is the historic expression of an elitist, colonialist, European society that doesn't recognize the validity of other ways of speaking English, such as that African-American dialect employed by Ms. Hansberry. I agree. As you've figured out by now, I like to write in a more-or-less conventional style; but I don't mistake my personal way of writing for the only correct way.

One of the reasons for the success of the English language is its constant adaptability and willingness to change.[53] Whatever enhances and clarifies your meaning is good writing, and whatever impedes it is bad writing. I suggest only that you be consistent; that you know your dialect well and use it respectfully; that you understand thoroughly the expressiveness of the style you have chosen; and that you don't write, spell or punctuate sloppily out of mere laziness.

The Eavesdropping Game

An acting teacher I know says that actors should never be ashamed to stare. If something interesting is happening on the street—even an altercation, which most people will turn away from in embarrassment or out of a reluctance to intrude—the actor has licence to watch and learn from it. Similarly, playwrights should never be ashamed to **eavesdrop**: to listen in on other conversations in a very specific way, which helps hone their dialogue skills.

To play the Eavesdropping game, go to a public place where people aren't especially quiet: a playground, a train station, a restaurant, a bar, a popular city square. Bring either a laptop or a pen and notebook, as well as a textbook. The textbook is a prop. As you sit there, scribbling or typing, stare conscientiously at your textbook, while actually listening to nearby conversations and writing them down as fast as you can. You can also do this casually through the day, by keeping a pen and small notebook with you to scribble down overheard lines.

This way of listening is analogous to the artist's technique of "sighting": looking at a model or a view not for "content," but as a

---

53 Another reason is that it was imposed on other countries by the forces of British imperialism.

collection of lines, angles, proportions, and perspectives. You listen more to *how* people are speaking than to *what* they say. Pay attention to the rhythms and, again, those little vocal encouragements we give each other. Notice how two or more people can talk at the same time and hear each other clearly; how people use different manners of speech to talk to different people; how they form long sentences and short sentences. What does a speaker's verbal style reveal about his background, his education, his attitude to life? What does it show about how she breathes, thinks, feels about the person she's talking to? Then, when you get your scribbled or typed dialogue home, do the second phase of the exercise: formatting, editing, and seeing how it looks as if it were a page of a script.

This exercise has built-in hazards and ethical requirements. Don't attract their attention, or let them know you're listening, by making eye contact, laughing, or responding in other ways. Don't eavesdrop on anyone you know personally, and, most importantly, be very wary of sharing your eavesdropped dialogue, and if you do, make sure it reveals nothing about anyone that might identify them.

Finally, be careful not to listen this way to conversation that's actually being spoken to you! You can get so preoccupied with how they're speaking that you stop hearing what they're saying. Suddenly they've asked you a question which you literally didn't hear, and everybody's waiting for your answer. The American humorist James Thurber wrote that his wife would sometimes come up to him at parties, having recognized a certain glazed look in his eyes, and hiss in his ear, "*Stop writing!*"

Control your cleverness

Never be clever
For the sake of being clever,
For the sake of showing off.
—"So you Want to Write a Fugue," a fugue with
lyrics by Glenn Gould, 1963

Beautiful writing is no excuse.
—Dr. Julie Salverson, Queen's University, in
conversation

Some playwrights fall into the trap of using dialogue to show the audience how clever they are. The audience wants—primarily—to see Characters facing Challenges, going through Changes and making Choices. Only briefly do they take an interest in the sets, costumes, lighting, incidental music, attractiveness of the actors, or your verbal cleverness as a playwright. When they do get distracted by such secondary entertainments, they'll soon be back to wanting to know what happens next—or let's hope they will! Even the cleverest of playwrights must, sooner or later, show us the souls of their characters, and cannot get by on wizardly stagecraft and verbal wordplay forever. With all due respect, neither can you.

During a performance, there's usually a moment about five to ten minutes in, when you can feel that the audience have figured out what the rules of tonight's game are, and you can sense them settling in to enjoy the story. After that, your cleverness won't impress them so much, as the surprise wears off. They'll want something more. If all you're showing them is cleverness, the laughs will dwindle, and you'll feel an unspoken message from the audience that says, "Okay, we know you're clever, what else you got?" And what they want from that point is to be taken along with the story, to get to know the characters, to be surprised—and to *feel* something.

PART 3

THE OTHER STUFF YOU DO ALONE

9

What Is This Thing Called Character?

> What your character *does* reveals who they are. What they
> *say* reveals who they see themself as.
>
> —Aaron Sorkin

Many books on fiction writing get a bit vague and philosophical when it comes to discussing that mysterious topic called "Character." Sad to report, so will this one. But it's a brief chapter and it will offer a few pointers.

It's brief because much of the work that creates character is described in other chapters. "Character"—what kinds of people your Characters are, how they talk and behave, what Changes they go through and Choices they make in response to the Challenges you set for them—appears in the interface between your plot and your dialogue, and can be expressed through plot, dialogue, or both. To put it another way, and to paraphrase Mr. Sorkin's excellent epigraph slightly: characters are what they do and what they say, and, to a lesser extent, what other people say *about* them and say or do *to* them.

Show, don't tell

You've probably encountered this piece of advice before. It's an oldie but a goodie. If you find yourself writing a lot of dialogue to persuade the audience that a character has certain characteristics, consider instead giving them one or two actions to demonstrate that characteristic. This can save you some unnecessary writing, and also the audience will believe it.

For example, William could have written much more dialogue in *Twelfth Night* for "Sir Toby and the lighter people," as Malvolio calls them, to chat about what a puritanical buzzkill he is. Instead, in Malvolio's first scene, when he's invited by Olivia to compliment Feste the court jester, he dismisses Feste's comedy with withering insults, and the viewers feel they know Malvolio already. This action has the added benefit of motivating Feste to join the others in humiliating him.

Ways to get to know your characters

There are numerous games and exercises you can do to help you get familiar with your characters. Here are a few.

In his *The Art of Dramatic Writing*, mentioned in Chapter 2, Lajos Egri writes, "Every object has three dimensions: depth, height, width. Human beings have an additional three dimensions: physiology, sociology, psychology."

He goes on to say that people with different physical appearances and abilities will see the world differently from each other; that "Sociology is the second dimension to be studied," and a person brought up in poverty will react differently than one brought up rich; and that "The third dimension, psychology, is the product of the other two. Their combined influence gives life to ambition, frustration, temperament, attitudes, complexes. Psychology, then, rounds out the three dimensions."

Egri then suggests ways to write out descriptions of your characters under more detailed sub-directories of these three categories. You can find this material in full, in *The Art of Dramatic Writing*

(New York: Touchstone Edition, 2004), pp. 34–35, followed by his suggested exercises.

Some other exercises for getting to know your characters are adapted from games and exercises originally devised for actors, but they can work equally well for playwrights. Here are a couple of those, which you might like to try.

• There are three versions of what's called the "Backstory" exercise, all written in the character's own voice. You can write the character's life story, from birth up to the first moment they appear in the play—or the story of what they've been doing for the 24 hours before their first appearance—and/or their activities between each exit and their subsequent entrance.

• Write a detailed physical description of the character and his/her/their clothing. If you like to draw, you might draw portraits of the character. But don't include this description in the script itself (unless there are details that are really necessary), and don't expect the director to cast an actor who resembles your physical description.

• Imagine that your character is a real person, living somewhere at a distance from you, who knows you're writing a play about them and has read all your work on it so far. Write the letter that the character would write you, telling you what they think of your work up to this point, and offering advice on how to proceed. (The character may or may not approve of how you're depicting them in the play.) Sometimes this exercise can provide you with advice you never thought of "on your own."

• I call this exercise "There's This Nurse," in honour of a funny exchange of dialogue in the movie *Shakespeare in Love* (1999), written by Marc Norman and Tom Stoppard. In a tavern, where the actors are relaxing after a day spent rehearsing their new tragedy *Romeo and Juliet*, a woman (Rachel Clark), drinking with the actor who plays the Nurse (Jim Carter), asks him, "What's the play about, then?" The actor replies, "Well, there's this nurse…."

We each picture ourselves as the hero of our own story. Every actor thinks about the play as if their own character were its protagonist. So take one of the least "important" characters in your play, and rewrite the plot outline as if they were the protagonist. How would *Romeo and Juliet* have looked if it had been called *Juliet's Nurse*? And how would your play look if it were all about that minor character? This exercise can teach you about not only that minor character, but the other characters as well; it sometimes even leads to revisions of plot.

• The "Kent Stetson Exercise" is named after the Montreal playwright, who suggested this during a visit to my Playwriting class at Queen's. Describe your character with three different monologues. Each of the first two monologues is by a different character or characters than the character you're describing. The third is by the character herself.

The first monologue is a description of your character, in the third person, by a speaker who does not know your character, but sees her walking down the street, and comments to someone else. The speaker can be a character you invent for the exercise, or another character in your play. You might imagine them sitting in a restaurant, looking out the window, and observing your character. They describe her physical appearance, behaviour, and/or clothing. Know when, in the timeline of the play, this monologue takes place.

The second monologue is by a person speaking *to* your character, making observations about her: "It seems to me that you..." "You have this weird habit of..." etc. This speaker may be the same one as in the previous monologue or may be someone else; may be in your play, or may not. But in this monologue, the speaker knows her personally, so now the observation has more to do with her personality, habits, patterns of behaviour, etc. Again, know when in the play this observation is being made.

And finally, for the third monologue, it's the character herself who is describing herself to another person. Again, know when she is making this speech. The person being spoken to may be the person who spoke in Part 1 or Part 2; may be another character in your play; or may not.

Contradictions and journeys

Sometimes, especially in the plot-cards stage, you may discover that a character is behaving differently in different parts of the play. It may serve your plot near the beginning of the play for them to be one kind of person, but towards the end, perhaps even forgetting you'd made that earlier decision, you've made them quite different. As with characters who "go rogue," you have options. You can change the character earlier, to match that character later—you can do the opposite—or you can see what happens if you keep both! Perhaps, in finding the Challenges and Choices that motivate the Character to Change from one condition to the other, you'll generate more plot.

A **journey** is a series of emotional Changes that a Character goes through, to get from one condition to another. One day in Playwriting class, I said, in this context, "A contradiction can sometimes lead you to a journey," and a young woman looked up at me with shining eyes and exclaimed, "John, that is *inspirational!*" It was one of those moments when I almost felt guilty for taking the university's money to do the job.

10

Exploiting the Limitations

"Piece out our imperfections with your thoughts"

> [L]et us, ciphers to this great accompt,
> On your imaginary forces work.
> Suppose within the girdle of these walls
> Are now confined two mighty monarchies,
> Whose high-uprearèd and abutting fronts
> The perilous narrow ocean parts asunder:
> Piece out our imperfections with your thoughts;
> Into a thousand parts divide one man,
> And make imaginary puissance;
> Think, when we talk of horses, that you see them
> Printing their proud hoofs i' the receiving earth;
> For 'tis your thoughts that now must deck our kings;
> Carry them here and there, jumping o'er times,
> Turning the accomplishment of many years
> Into an hour-glass.
>
> —Prologue, *Henry V*, William Shakespeare

This is part of the speech that begins William's history play about King Henry V, who lived about 200 years before William wrote it. You may have recognized it and may already know what it means. If not, here's a quick rundown:

The character speaking these lines is the Chorus, who is acting as an intermediary between the play and the audience. In the earlier part of the speech, before the above excerpt, he complains of their theatre's lack of resources worthy to tell the story of this great warrior-king. He apologizes to the audience for "The flat unraisèd spirits that have dared / On this unworthy scaffold to bring forth / So great an object" as Henry V. "Can this cock-pit hold / The vasty fields of France?" Clearly representing William himself, he even bemoans his own lack of inventiveness!

But then he comes up with a solution: *let us on your imaginary forces work. Suppose...*

He invites the audience to imagine along with the actors: that within the girdle of these walls stand the mighty monarchies of England and France, with the perilously narrow English Channel between them. He asks us to "Piece out [their] imperfections with [our] thoughts." He asks us to help create imaginary power ("puissance"); to pretend that one man onstage is a thousand, and thus to create an imaginary army; to think, when they mention horses, that we see them, printing their proud hooves in the earth; and to decorate the kings onstage with our thoughts, and turn the achievements of many years into the events of an hour.

His frustration may seem familiar to the present-day playwright. Nowadays, though, we may yearn for the money they have on Broadway or in Hollywood: the expensive sets, the big casts— and in movies, the gorgeous locations, the thousands of extras, and then the imagery-generating computer programs so that we wouldn't need all that other stuff. Well, this passage from 1599 or thereabouts indicates that that frustration over our limited means is not a new feeling.

But it also indicates what we playwrights, often working in small theatres with limited resources, *can* do: invite the audience to imagine along with us. The solution is to exploit those very limitations and turn them into an advantage. That's not just a poor second to the resources of big movies: it is an attribute of live theatre which movies cannot duplicate. What may seem at first to be limitations can create opportunities for a kind of expression that you can't achieve on film.

Film audiences don't expect to piece out the movie's imperfections. In the movie theatre, we want to see everything. We think of movies as reality seen through a frame, and theatre as action on a stage representing some other reality. Theatre has one other added advantage: the actors are in the same room with us and can hear and feel our responses, so that we interact with them—which also helps to build the reality of the play with our thoughts.

The late actor Christopher Plummer spoke eloquently of the contribution of the audience's imagination, in a 2016 interview with journalist Peter Mansbridge on CBC Television:

> It happens in the movies, but mostly in the theatre, and when it works in the theatre, it's absolutely wonderful, because you've used your imagination. It hasn't all been spelled out for you, as movies can do. It's the job of movies to visualize everything, so nothing is left to the imagination, and in the theatre it's the other way around, and when it works, it's wonderful.[54]

Transparent symbolism

The secret to recruiting the audience's imagination is to show them *how* you're doing the trick *while* you're doing the trick, so that they have a sort of double vision: seeing the effect, while also seeing how it's done. I call this "transparent symbolism," because the symbolism is there, but we can see through it to the visible technique.

As a playwright, you don't *need* to employ transparent symbolism in the plays you write—there's nothing wrong with realistic plays which simply show us what we're meant to see—but it's a versatile technique which can come in handy when you're trying to present something onstage which cannot really be presented onstage.

In a sense, all theatre is transparent symbolism. We know we're watching a play, and we're willing to play along. Samuel Taylor Coleridge called this "the willing suspension of disbelief for the moment, which constitutes poetic faith." In her book *Insecurity:*

---

54 https://www.youtube.com/watch?v=xaM0I0hEBzU&t=12s, 11:17

Perils and Products of Theatres of the Real, Jenn Stephenson expands on Coleridge's description:

> Entry into the fictional world is a determined act. In addition to the purposeful adoption of this new perspective, Coleridge asserts that the audience always retains cognitive possession of their former perceptions as well. Both actual and fictional phenomena are held in balance through a kind of binocular vision.[55]

Transparent symbolism with masks, puppets, etc.

With masks and puppets, transparent symbolism has often been used to represent animals onstage, with the human manipulators clearly visible, sometimes inside the animal costumes. Perhaps the best-known example (and one which proves that the technique is not new) is in *A Midsummer-Night's Dream,* when Nick Bottom is magically given the head of an ass—and when it is later removed, in full view of the audience. In fact, earlier in *Dream,* the labourers rehearsing their own play, *Pyramus and Thisbe,* experiment with transparent symbolism themselves. When they worry that Snug, playing the Lion, might frighten the ladies, Bottom suggests that half his face be seen through the lion's neck, and that he explain that he's actually just a harmless human named Snug.

Such symbolism has been used to represent horses, in Peter Shaffer's *Equus* (1973) and the National Theatre of Great Britain's 2007 stage production of *War Horse,* adapted by Nick Stafford from the novel by Michael Morpurgo. The National Theatre more recently used life-sized animal puppets to great effect in their 2019 production of *The Life of Pi,* written by Lolita Chakrabarti from the novel by Yann Martel.

Closer to home, with less fame but at least equal charm, the Caravan Farm Theatre of Armstrong, B.C. produced a comedy in 1981 by Peter Anderson and Phil Savath, called *Horseplay.* The horse characters were represented by actors in masks designed and built by Melody Anderson, with the actors' faces visible within the open fronts of the

---

55 Jenn Stephenson, *Insecurity: Perils and Products of Theatres of the Real* (Toronto: University of Toronto Press, 2019), 11.

horses' necks. The Caravan Farm Theatre is both an outdoor theatre company and a working farm, and Ms. Anderson writes:

> When Laddie, the Caravan's resident Clydesdale stud, saw the actors wearing the masks he took off at a gallop, kicking and snorting—a reaction I still consider to be one of the highest compliments my work has received. The Caravan horses soon became used to their two-legged companions.[56]

In Colleen Murphy's *The Breathing Hole / Aglu*, the lead character is a 500-year-old one-eared polar bear named Anguřuaq. In the 2018 Stratford (Ontario) Festival production, he was designed by Daniela Marsellis, built in the Stratford shop with lead builder Michelle Jamieson, and "played" by a manipulator clearly visible under a life-sized puppet made of white cloth fitted over a wire framework. I confess that, sitting in the front row at a performance, I felt a *frisson* of nerves when this imposing beast padded closely by me.

Most famously, there's *The Lion King*, directed and designed for the Broadway stage by Julie Taymor, so that, again, the audience can see both the human actors and their animal characters, and there's no attempt to trick us into thinking, as the characters in *Dream* fear their audience might think, that those are real lions up there. Taymor explained to the nervous Disney producers, "My audience knows it's a theatre."

The effect on the audience is a kind of double vision. On the one hand you're seeing an overtly fake animal's head sitting on top of a real actor's head. Then you blink and you're seeing the animal. And you keep going back and forth like that.

In the revered Japanese *bunraku*—puppet theatre for all ages, regarded as high art, with a long history of respected traditions—the puppeteers are always in full view of the audience. And similarly, Toronto's Ronnie Burkett remains in full audience view, as he walks around on the stage with his marionettes while manipulating their strings and speaking all their lines. With both bunraku and Burkett, one goes from watching puppeteers manipulating their

---

56 Melody Anderson, *Making Masks* (Vancouver: self-published on Blurb, 2022), 34.

toys to suddenly feeling half-convinced that the puppets are live actors, with titans hovering behind them.

The Elephant Man is the title of both a 1977 play written by Bernard Pomerance and a 1980 movie written by Christopher De Vore, Eric Bergren, and David Lynch, and directed by Mr. Lynch. Both are excellent fictional treatments of the same true story, of Joseph Merrick (1862–1890), one of the most deformed people in history. Merrick's skull was large and misshapen, his skin thick and lumpy, and the rest of his body beset with other deformities.

The movie and the play approach the story very differently. Filmmaker David Lynch used makeup and prostheses to turn actor John Hurt into a realistic facsimile of the actual Merrick. But playwright Pomerance has Merrick played by a handsome young man, who distorts his face and body but wears no special makeup. (The role has been played by, among other actors, David Bowie in 1980 and Bradley Cooper in 2015.)

So throughout the play, we see the actor both as he really looks to us—and as Joseph Merrick would have looked if the universe had been fair to him—and as he looked in reality, judging from the responses of the characters around him, and from onstage projections. This gives us a kind of double vision which adds poignancy to the event: transparent symbolism at its best.[57]

Transparent symbolism with doubling and other casting devices

Even the simple device of **doubling**—having an actor play more than one character within the same play—can convey added meaning. In 1990 I wrote a play called *Homework for Men*, about a middle-aged man in conflict with his teenage son. The father

---

57 There have been at least two other adaptations of Merrick's story that show him "realistically." In the 1989 comedy movie *The Tall Guy*, Jeff Goldblum plays an actor who gets cast as the lead in a musical about Merrick, wearing facial prostheses which start to fall off as he sings and dances on opening night. And in 2002, French composer Edmund Petitgirard and librettist Eric Nonn wrote an opera, *Joseph Merrick The Elephant Man*, in which the lead singer, a contralto, actually does wear a latex mask and partial body suit. It is not reported that anything fell off during the first production (Prague, 2002), but reviews were mixed.

remembers similar conflicts with his own middle-aged father when he himself was a teenager. We had two actors—one in his 40s and one in his 20s—playing the present-day father and his present-day son, and doubling as the father's younger self and his own middle-aged dad. A theme of the play—that, when dealing with our children, we tend to echo our parents—was expressed poignantly by having each actor play two generations of fathers and sons: an example of how supposed limitations can actually provide more opportunities for expression.

Some standard conventions in casting qualify as transparent symbolism but are so familiar that we often fail to notice them. In William's theatre, with female characters played by men, the audience had the double vision of seeing love stories "lived" by a male and female character but performed by two men. These days we often see the reverse, with women playing traditionally male roles in William's plays, or with "gender-blind" casting generally. This is not that new an innovation: "trouser roles," as they were called, were popular in 19th-century opera, and in 1899, Sarah Bernhardt caused a sensation as Hamlet, both for being the first woman to play the role, and for playing the 30-year-old prince at the age of 55.

Today we also have a relatively new example of transparent symbolism in casting: actors of colour cast in classical plays in the Western canon. As far as is known, the earliest evidence of a Black actor on the English stage is a 1793 engraving by William Hogarth.[58] Black actors were probably not cast in William's plays during his era, not even as the specifically Black characters in *Othello, The Merchant of Venice,* and *Titus Andronicus.*

Sometimes this kind of casting is described as **colour-blind**, meaning that we ignore the fact that (for example) a Black actor is playing a traditionally white role. And sometimes, by means of context or of cultural clues such as costuming, the actor is understood to be playing the character *as* a Black character. Similarly, as mentioned above, a female actor might play a traditionally male character as a man—as Bernhardt played Hamlet—or she might (sometimes with minor alterations in

---

58 https://mancunion.com/2020/10/16/the-history-of-black-theatre-in-britain/

the text) play the character as a Lady Polonius, Princess Hamlet, Duchess Prospero or Queen Lear.

Small casts, few sets

In 1913, in New York City, a group of American actors got together and formed a labour union, the Actors' Equity Association. British Actors' Equity followed suit in 1930. Canadian actors formed our own branch of American Equity in 1955, and then broke off (politely, of course) to form the Canadian Actors' Equity Association in 1974.

Part of the purpose of Equity was to introduce the radical notion that actors should be paid a living wage. And one of the results of this was that—as you'll see if you look at scripts from before and after the forming of Actors' Equity Associations in their respective countries—casts suddenly got a whole lot smaller, as actors got more expensive. Currently, in most professional Canadian theatres, a cast of six or seven actors is considered a large cast.

So write for small casts. Make sure you're not putting two or three characters onstage to do a job that one can do. If your story really needs a larger cast, look for ways your actors can double. And similarly, try to limit the number of different settings called for in your script.

Once again, there are exceptions. My most-frequently-produced play, *Village of Idiots* (1985), features 16 characters, plus villagers and soldiers as needed. However, as I'm careful to point out on the script's Introductory page, it can be produced with as few as seven or eight actors, with multiple casting. It's also worth mentioning that many productions of *Village* are by amateur companies and student groups, which often welcome larger-cast scripts. Even so, I'd advise against writing a play with a deliberately large cast, in the hopes of getting a lot of community and student productions. Even for those groups, 16 characters is a demanding number. It may even be difficult for the audience to get to know that many characters in their brief allotted amounts of stage time. And I must add that my *second*-most-frequently-produced play, *Babel Rap*, boasts a cast of two. So as a general rule, think in terms of a small cast, on an easy-to-manipulate set.

In praise of black boxes and storefronts

Finally on this topic, this is a good place to mention the smaller theatre venues, because it is in them, with their more limited physical resources, that transparent symbolism is often most effective. Some people who have not worked at or attended very much theatre think that the only theatres worth taking seriously are those large-capacity **proscenium** houses: theatres with the stage positioned so that the audience all faces in the same direction, and featuring a **proscenium arch**, that big archway that divides the audience from the stage and usually contains a curtain. Such theatres traditionally feature plenty of red velvet, gold paint, and carved wood.

Between the Restoration period and the 1950s, almost every professional theatre venue in the West was of this type. These days they are typically the homes for the kinds of large-scale shows, especially musicals, that you'll find on Broadway, in London's West End, or, in Canada, under the management of such companies as Mirvish Productions.

Now this is not to express any prejudice against those big, beautiful houses or the kinds of shows presented in them! I've had delightful experiences in rooms like that, and I hope you have too, or that you will. But theatregoers whose experience is limited to those spaces may not know that theatres now come in many shapes and sizes. If you make your career in the theatre, you may find yourself spending much or most of your time in venues at the smaller end of the scale: those so-called "black boxes" or "storefront theatres," which seat audiences numbered in the dozens instead of the hundreds or thousands.

A **black box** is what it sounds like: a square or rectangular room, painted black, and usually with **flexible seating**, which means the directors and designers can move the seats to place the audience differently for different productions: proscenium-style, **in the round**, in **corridor seating**, or with a **thrust stage**. Theatre in the round places the stage in the middle of the room and the audience on all sides of it. (The shape of the stage isn't necessarily round.) Corridor seating places the stage, usually a rectangle, between two sections of audience which face each other. A thrust stage has the audience on three sides of it, so that it "thrusts" into the house.

(You should know these terms, but it's rare for playwrights to specify which kind of seating they want: that's usually the decision of the director and designers.)

A **storefront theatre** is also what it sounds like: a theatre built inside a former store on a commercial city street—and, yes, an average-sized store makes for a pretty small theatre, so many storefront theatres are also black boxes.

Working in these small theatres, and writing for them, offers its own particular rewards. There are possibilities for staging unavailable in the bigger houses. And, of course, there's a special kind of intimacy in having a small audience whose members are sitting so close to the actors. **Fringe festivals**, a popular annual home for cutting-edge theatre in many large Canadian cities, depend almost entirely on productions on this scale.

Some theatre doesn't take place in theatres at all but depends for part of its meaning on its non-traditional setting, which has a significance of its own. This is **site-specific theatre**, and it usually accommodates only small audiences. **Immersive theatre** goes further and is designed for audiences of as few as one or two people per performance, who are, as the name suggests, "immersed" in the production rather than observing it from the outside.

Regarding smaller houses in general, there seems to be a persistent public opinion that the seriously talented artists work in the big plush palaces (as, of course, many of them do), while those who toil in the smaller venues are doing so because they, or we, aren't good enough for the big time—whereas, in fact, talented professionals work in houses of all sizes.

I'll close this chapter with a quotation from the late Charles Ludlam, a New York actor, director, playwright, artistic director of the New York Theatre of the Ridiculous, and all-round genius. In 1975 Ludlam wrote a "Manifesto," part of which reads: "The theatre is a humble materialist enterprise which seeks to produce riches of the imagination, not the other way around. The theatre is an event and not an object. Theatre workers need not blush and conceal their desperate struggle to pay the landlords their rents."[59]

---

59 https://www.contrib.andrew.cmu.edu/~norm/manifesto.html

11

The Stuff That Isn't Dialogue

Narration on the Stage, Directions on the Page

Having looked at dialogue earlier, let's now look at the forms of non-dialogue which also appear in scripts. Some of it is spoken onstage and some is not.

The spoken stuff comprises direct address to the audience—**narration, soliloquies,** and **asides**—and we'll also look at **monologues**, though in fact monologues are dialogue with one character doing all the talking. And the unspoken stuff, which shows up in scripts but is *not* spoken onstage, consists of **character descriptions, set descriptions,** and **stage directions.** Finally, we'll take a brief look at **titles**.

But as we begin with *spoken* non-dialogue, here's a strong suggestion:

Avoid it

My playwriting classes for beginners feature a rule against all forms of direct address to the audience: narration, soliloquies, and asides. Every word spoken in my beginning students' plays must be spoken *by* a character—which means no chorus, storyteller, or narrator—and *to* a character—which means no soliloquies or asides. However, monologues to other characters are permitted (see below), and in my intermediate and advanced playwriting courses, the rule no longer applies, on the assumption that by now the students have some grasp on how to tell their stories without these devices.

But if you're starting out at this, you might want to apply my rule against direct address to your own work. There are two reasons for this rule.

One is that, as stated in Chapter 1, the playwright's task is to sneak the story across to the audience by means of characters who don't know that there is a story to tell or an audience to hear it. It's the beginner's job to learn how to do this, by getting used to the fact that (here we go again) every line should have both a storyteller's reason and a character's reason for existing. A soliloquy or aside fulfills the storyteller's reason, which is to inform the audience, but there's no character's reason.

The other reason for this rule is that when beginners have the option of letting a character simply turn to the audience and explain what's going on, they tend to rely on that easy option and resort to blatant narration, rather than letting the play unfold through the actions of the characters.

Having said all this, I should add that many playwriting teachers disagree with this rule against narration, soliloquies, and asides. In fact, some very fine instructors have their students writing soliloquies near the beginning of their playwriting courses, and then using them as the foundations for their plays.

In any case, even if you choose to wait to try these forms of direct address until after you've learned to do without them, you should still know about them, so here we go:

The narrator or chorus

Narration consists of a character telling the audience what's going on, rather than (or in addition to) letting us see it onstage for ourselves. The narrator used to be, and sometimes still is, called a **chorus**, as in the Prologue from William's *Henry V*, quoted in the previous chapter, in which the Chorus goes on to say, "Admit me Chorus to this history."

In Western theatre, the earliest chori (Latin plural of "chorus") show up in Ancient Athenian plays, in the form of a group of actors, often speaking in unison, who, back then, were not narrators but characters within the play, representing onstage the community of the audience.

By William's era, the chorus was usually one actor, who was not a character within the play but stood outside it, knowing it's a play and commenting on it to the audience. William also added **epilogues** to a few of his plays, in which characters in the play suddenly step out of it at the end to become themselves, mere actors, now knowing that it's a play and humbly requesting our applause and good will.

In more recent times, the narrator or chorus is a less frequent device, but has turned up occasionally—sometimes as a character who comes out of the play and addresses the audience—as in Jean Anouilh's *Antigone* (1942), Tennessee Williams' *The Glass Menagerie* (1944), Max Frisch's *The Firebugs* (1953), and Thornton Wilder's *Our Town* (1938) and *The Skin of Our Teeth* (1942).

The soliloquy

Unlike a chorus, the speaker of a **soliloquy** is a character in the play, who does *not* know that they're in a play, and yet, strangely enough, is able to speak to the audience.

Hamlet's Act 2, Scene 2 soliloquy, commonly known by its supposed first line, "O what a rogue and peasant slave am I," actually begins with the words, "Now I am alone"—not "Now I am alone with all you lovely ladies and gentlemen." And in the scene right after that, he speaks the most famous soliloquy ever written, "To be or not to be"—this time definitely not alone, even within the world of the play, but with three other characters spying on him, just offstage. After he's done that soliloquy and has then ranted at poor Ophelia and left her weeping on the floor, the other two spies enter—Claudius and Polonius—and Polonius says, "We heard it all." And yet none of them mentions that Hamlet, whose state of mind all three are obsessed with for different reasons, has just been talking out loud, for 33 lines of iambic pentameter, about whether or not to kill himself. That's because they *didn't* hear that part. That's the nature of soliloquy.

Soliloquies seldom contain plot information: what they're usually about is the current emotional state of the character. In a sense, the job of the soliloquy is to reveal subtext: the hidden emotions and opinions that the character is not revealing to anybody else. Hamlet doesn't share with any other characters his idea that to be or not to be is the only question in life; he shares it only with the audience.

Indigenous playwrights, coming as they do from a tradition steeped in storytelling, are introducing interesting innovations to the soliloquy form. For example, in *My Sister's Rage* (2022), Yolanda Bonnell features a character who appears to be an ordinary, if perhaps demented, old lady, but is later revealed to be an incarnation of Nanabush, the Trickster / Creator figure in Ojibwe mythology. Her speeches are part chorus and part soliloquy; she even leads the audience in howling like wolves and hooting like owls. Anishinaabe playwright Waawaate Fobister does something similar in his play *Agokwe*, with Nanabush again—this time explicitly using that name—serving as a chorus to that play.[60]

The aside

The **aside** is a sort of miniature soliloquy of just a few words, spoken to the audience, usually while the character is in the middle of a dialogue with other characters. The convention is that the other characters don't hear it. William's dialogue is full of asides—or passages that actors can, and often do, choose to speak as asides, though they were not identified as such with the stage direction "*(Aside:)*" until the 18th century.

There are already examples of asides in this book. One is in Chapter 7, from *Romeo and Juliet*: Tybalt's explanation to the

---

60 Waawaate Fobister, *Agokwe,* in *Two-Spirit Acts: Queer Indigenous Performances*, ed. Jean O'Hara (Toronto: Playwrights Canada Press, 2013).

audience about why he is trembling. And in this excerpt from Kathleen Oliver's *Swollen Tongues*, first quoted in Chapter 2 and repeated here, Catherine has two asides in a row, which Sonja does not hear even though she's close enough to be measuring her for a new dress:

> CATHERINE: *(Aside.)* How near to truth her blithe fantasy hits!
>
> SONJA: Hold still, Catherine! I can't tell if this fits...
> The bust is much too big. It needs a dart...
>
> CATHERINE: *(Aside.)* Her hands upon my breast! Be still my heart!

The monologue

The **monologue** is simply a longer-than-usual, uninterrupted bit of text, spoken by one character to another or others. It doesn't really belong on the current list—it is not a form of direct address to the audience—but it is included here because people often confuse it with the soliloquy. During a monologue, another character might interrupt at any moment but chooses not to do so. In a sense, a monologue is dialogue, with the other characters contributing silence. So the definition is subjective: there's no hard-and-fast length, or official word count, at which an ordinary speech becomes a "monologue."

Character descriptions and set descriptions

The Reverend James Mavor Morell is a Christian Socialist clergyman of the Church of England, and an active member of the Guild of St. Matthew and the Christian Social Union. A vigorous, genial, popular man of forty, robust and goodlooking, full of energy, with pleasant, hearty, considerate manners, and a sound unaffected voice, which he uses with the clean athletic articulation of a practised orator, and with a wide range and perfect command of expression. He is a first rate clergyman, able to say what he likes to whom he likes, to lecture people without setting himself up against them, to impose his authority on them without humiliating them, and, on occasion, to interfere in their business without impertinence. His well-spring of enthusiasm and sympathetic emotion has never run dry for a moment: he still eats and sleeps heartily enough to win the daily battle between exhaustion and recuperation triumphantly. Withal, a great baby, pardonably vain of his powers and unconsciously pleased with himself. He has a healthy complexion: good forehead, with the brows somewhat blunt, and the eyes bright and eager, mouth resolute but not particularly well cut, and a substantial nose, with the mobile spreading nostrils of the dramatic orator, void, like all his features, of subtlety.

—Character description of James Morrell,
Candida, George Bernard Shaw, 1895

SAM, thirty-five
Shaved head. Caucasian.
He often wears a beat-up Red Sox cap.
He used to be very into Heavy Metal.

AVERY, twenty
African-American. Bespectacled.
He wears red slightly European-looking sneakers.
In love with the movies.

ROSE, twenty-four
Caucasian. Sexually magnetic, despite the fact that (or partly because?) her clothes are baggy, she never wears makeup and her hair is dyed forest-green.

SKYLAR / THE DREAMING MAN, twenty-six

—The complete descriptions of the entire cast of
The Flick, Annie Baker, 2014[61]

---

61 Annie Baker, *The Flick* (New York: Theatre Communications Group, 2014), 4–5.

So what happened there? It looks as though, at some time in the 119 years between *Candida* and the Pulitzer-Prize-winning *The Flick*, character descriptions mostly dried up and blew away. So did set descriptions and stage directions, which also used to be much more discursive than they are now: Shaw's description of Morrell is just part of his 900-word description of the Northeast London neighbourhood, the house, and the room onstage, in which the play takes place.

In fact, this change in styles of setting and character descriptions took place in a relatively short time: as late as the 1960s, Tennessee Williams' and Arthur Miller's setting and character descriptions resembled Shaw's more than Baker's in their verbosity. To examine why they changed after that, let's start with a closer look at those old-fashioned styles.

When Shaw wrote *Candida*, there was no such official designation as "director." Often the playwrights conducted the rehearsals of their own plays, doing the kind of work that directors do now, including casting. So Shaw was probably describing a specific actor whom he had in mind. However, as a present-day playwright whose plays are cast and directed by others, you can be pretty sure that if you write into the script that your lead character is tall, thin, and black-haired, the director will cast a short, rotund, blond actor who will be perfect for the part! Unless you have a specific reason to demand a specific type, writing a physical description unnecessarily limits your casting possibilities—and maybe even the play's chances for production.

Set descriptions, too, used to run to great lengths but now tend to be minimal. As mentioned above, Shaw's description of Morell is only a fraction of his longer description of the set and setting; Tennessee Williams' set description for *A Streetcar Named Desire* (1947) is similarly long and detailed, running to 283 words; and *A Raisin in the Sun*, Lorraine Hansberry's ground-breaking 1959 drama of African-American family life in Southside Chicago, opens with a 542-word description of the setting and of the character Ruth. By contrast, the entire set description for David Mamet's *Oleanna* (1993) reads, "The play takes place in John's office."

Stage directions: "With a tear in his eye," etc.

There's another area where formerly verbose descriptions have dwindled away in the last 50 years. Twentieth-century American playwrights in particular included stage directions, scattered through the dialogue, describing the characters' physical gestures and inner feelings. Here's a passage from Hansberry's *A Raisin in the Sun* (1958), in which a cheque for $10,000 U.S., paying off the life insurance on the family's deceased patriarch, arrives at the Younger household. For a struggling family, this would have been life-changing money in an era when, according to the play, $3,500 was a down payment on a three-bedroom house in a desirable Chicago neighbourhood.

(The bell sounds suddenly and sharply and all three are stunned—serious and silent—in mid-speech. In spite of all the other conversations and distractions of the morning, this is what they have been waiting for, even TRAVIS, who looks helplessly from his mother to his grandmother. RUTH is the first to come to life again.)

RUTH: *(To TRAVIS.)* Get down them steps, boy! *(TRAVIS snaps to life and flies out to get the mail.)*

MAMA: *(Her eyes wide, her hand to her breast.)* You mean it done really come?

RUTH: *(Excited.)* Oh, Miss Lena!

MAMA: *(Collecting herself.)* Well...I don't know what we all so excited about 'round here for. We known it was coming for months.

RUTH: That's a whole lot different from having it come and being able to hold it in your hands... a piece of paper worth ten thousand dollars... *(TRAVIS bursts back into the room. He holds the envelope high above his head, like a little dancer, his face is radiant and he is breathless. He moves to his grandmother with sudden slow ceremony and puts the envelope into her hands. She accepts it, and then merely holds it and looks at it.)* Come on! Open it... [...]

(MAMA finally makes a good strong tear and pulls out the thin blue slice of paper and inspects it closely. The boy and his mother study it raptly over MAMA's shoulder.) […]

MAMA: *(She holds the check away from her, still looking at it. Slowly her face sobers into a mask of unhappiness.)* Ten thousand dollars. *(She hands it to RUTH.)* Put it away somewhere, Ruth. *(She does not look at RUTH: her eyes seem to be seeing something somewhere very far off.)* Ten thousand dollars they give you. Ten thousand dollars.[62]

These are beautiful stage directions, and directors and actors could do worse than to pay close attention to them. There is great charm in the description of little Travis presenting his grandmother with the cheque. But if a cast rehearsed with all those directions removed from the scripts,[63] they would still find those shadings that Hansberry describes, for the dialogue itself supplies them. Good dialogue inspires good acting.

The decline of descriptions and directions

That 19th- and 20th-century style seems to have worked to everyone's satisfaction at the time. My theory is that their decline over the last 60 years is linked to the growing acceptance of Method acting. The Stanislavski Method has a lot to do with analyzing what the character wants and how the character is going about getting it, rather than, say, displaying the facial expression dictated by the script. So these days, those kinds of written directions may be seen as an attempt to tell the actor how to do their job.

So if, as a playwright, you are tempted to write:

---

62 Lorraine Hansberry, *A Raisin in the Sun* (New York: Signet Books, 1958), 54–56.

63 This comment on removing stage directions isn't just theoretical. Sad to say, some actors actually do that: open a new script they've never seen before, go through it and cross out all the stage directions without reading them. This is unfortunate, and disrespectful to the playwright. In any era, there may well be directions in there that the actor is going to need.

FRED: *(With a tear in his eye and a catch in his voice, knowing he's never going to see her again and this is their last moment together.)* Yes.

—then you may want to cut that stage direction and replace that "Yes" with a different line of dialogue, written in such a way that in rehearsal, the actor playing Fred suddenly has a tear in his eye and a catch in his voice, etc. And if he doesn't, maybe it's time for a rewrite.

Of course, by *not* writing those directions, you take the "risk" that they'll come up with something very different—but that can be a great thing. Those written directions might inhibit the actors from finding interpretations you hadn't thought of. Indeed, sometimes students and beginners virtually impose bad acting with stage directions like *"Yelling at the top of his lungs."* In such cases I like to ask the actor to do the exact opposite to what the stage directions demands. The results are often startlingly effective.

The way to discover the optimum interpretation for a specific cast is simply by trying them out in rehearsal. If you watch different productions of the same play, you'll see how widely interpretations of the same text can differ. You can, in fact, try this at home, by watching different movie adaptations of the same stage play.

It must be added that there are, as with everything, exceptions to this advice against detailed stage directions—particularly physical theatre, involving dance, mime, and movement.

Those other stage directions: "Cross D.L.C., turn R.," etc.

Another kind of stage direction which has also become obsolete is those indications of **blocking**—the physical positioning of the actors on the stage—which were popular in scripts in pamphlet form published by the American organizations the Dramatists Play Service and Samuel French, Inc., between the 1940s and 1970s: "Turning R." "Leaning against D.S. end of table." "She runs to R. door and opens it, keeping her L. hand on outside doorknob."[64] Etc.

---

64 These are real stage directions from an actual Broadway play of the 1940s.

154 *TWO WAYS ABOUT IT*

These kinds of directions seem to have come from the practice of borrowing the stage manager's prompt script, created during the rehearsals of the play, and copying everything in it: after all, it was the most up-to-date version of the play. (Many of those published scripts also contain the props list, set diagrams, and photographs from the original production.) As a result of this practice, the casts of subsequent productions would slavishly imitate the stage directions that had worked well for the original cast, whether or not they worked for others.

In addition, some playwrights came to think it was part of their job to create blocking and business for actors they didn't know, to perform on sets as yet un-designed, on stages they'd never seen. This belief was exacerbated somewhat by the 19th- and early-20th-century practice, mentioned above, of playwrights directing their own plays and, sometimes, designing their own sets.

The fact is that you and I, at our laptops or notebooks, cannot imagine the ways that real actors are going to move through that real space—or, at least, not as well as they can when they're in the room among their colleagues. Let them do that part. Your job is the words.

Titles

You probably want a brief and memorable title. Long, awkward titles seem to be a specialty of inexperienced playwrights, while more seasoned writers go in for the briefer, easier-to-remember ones. My recent titles include *Exposure*, *Meltdown*, and *The Grandkid*. My first produced play, mentioned in Chapter 2, was called *Chester, You Owe My Bird an Apology*. In addition to its being cumbersome, hard to remember, and uninformative about the play, it also gave one critic the ammo for this little burn from the first review I ever got as a playwright: "There's more than the bird deserving of an apology."[65]

Exceptions to this short-title guideline tend to be avant-garde or at least eccentric, as with Peter Weiss's supremely strange and

---

65 Don Hunter, "Chilliwack Scores High, Low," *Vancouver Province*, Apr. 20, 1972.

wonderful play *The Persecution and Assassination of Jean-Paul Marat as Performed by the Inmates of the Asylum at Charenton under the Direction of the Marquis de Sade* (1963), popularly (and understandably) shortened to *Marat / Sade*.[66] There's also the memorably weird title of Arthur Kopit's first play, also first produced in 1963: *Oh Dad, Poor Dad, Mamma's Hung You in the Closet and I'm Feelin' So Sad: A Pseudoclassical Tragifarce in a Bastard French Tradition*, similarly popularly shortened, in this case to its first four words. To get away with titles like these, you'd better be confident that your play is out there on the cutting edge.

Titles cannot be copyrighted, so if you use a title that's been used by someone else, they can't make trouble for you, or vice versa. *Two Ways About It* is also the title of an American novel for young readers by Judy Frank Mearian (Dial, 1985). However, you do want something unique and memorable which others are unlikely to think of. One approach is to go through the script, looking for an unusual phrase that might jump out as useful. That's where I got *Totally Nana's Ride* and *Medea's Disgust*. (This process can also be cheated: you can come up with an odd, interesting phrase, and then work it into the text, as an excuse to make it the title.) Another approach is to look to other great literature for quotes: William and the Bible have provided thousands of titles for other works. And a third approach is to think about what is central to the play: what's it about, at its core? That's where we got the title for *Dreaming and Duelling*.

---

66 It seems even more forbidding in the original German in which Weiss wrote it: *Die Verfolgung und Ermordung Jean Paul Marats dargestellt durch die Schauspielgruppe des Hospizes zu Charenton unter Anleitung des Herrn de Sade.*

12

Organizing and Formatting

Oh, is this chapter not creative enough for you?

Don't kid yourself that there's a difference between the part of the work that the audience will recognize as creative and artistic, and the simple grunt work of getting the details right. The seasoned playwright will take a moment, while struggling with the deepest questions of theme or character, to fix a comma that's in the wrong place. The more you work in any art form, the clearer it becomes that there is no real dividing line between profound artistry and small details of presentation—or if there is, it's a waste of time and energy to try to decide where that line goes. So let's talk about formatting.

Keeping organized for yourself

Later in this chapter, I'll suggest ways to make your play presentable and professional-looking to other readers. This first part is about how to keep your drafts organized for yourself. Different writers have different ways to do this, and you will evolve your own, but notes describing my methods may be a useful starting point. Paying attention to this mundane stuff early on might save you from much more frustrating, tedious work later.

For one thing, however messy and disorganized your writing room may be—if a typhoon hit it, leaving loose pages from a dozen drafts of a dozen different plays lying randomly everywhere—you want to be able to pick up a single sheet and know which page it is, from which draft of which play. So get to know your running-heads, or, as they're known in some word-processing programs, headers and footers. Learn how to use your computer's version of these, to place the title, your name, the draft number and the page number at the top of each page.

You might write notes to yourself, within the body of the draft, for changes you want to make later. I've created a macro that puts a tilde and the date at the beginning. The tilde is that Spanish diacritical that shows up in words like "señor" and "mañana," and I use it with Search and Replace, because I rarely use it at any other time. So my notes to myself look like the sentence below. They're easy to find by eye or by Search and Replace, and the date is there because sometimes it's useful to know which notes were written most recently.

> ~ January 20, 2022. Come back later and make this character a chain-smoker.

For what it's worth, I have other personal symbols: three ampersands—&&&—before and after a passage that's been pasted into the middle of a scene, but which may need to be smoothed around the edges; and three "at" symbols—@@@—to indicate where I left off last time.

By the way, my notes to myself are so detailed that I get embarrassed by their nerditude when other people read them. But you might get called away from a project for weeks or months, and it's frustrating to return to it and no longer understand your own notes. So I write mine as if they were addressed to someone else.

There's an art (well, a craft) to taking the notes you've written down during a workshop or a rehearsal and working them into your existing draft. We'll look at that in Chapter 14, on workshops and related activities.

Files and directories

You may find it useful to keep a directory called "Plays-Unproduced," and—I hope, as your career progresses—another called "Plays-Produced." Within them, each play has its own sub-directory. Within those, let's say for a play called *Totally Nana's Ride*, there are the drafts: "Nanas-Dr-01.docx,"[67] "Nanas-Dr-02.docx," etc. There are also individual files of the notes written on each draft for the next one, called "Nanas-Nts-01-02.docx," etc., meaning notes *on* the first draft, *for* the second draft.

If you're a true obsessive about this, like oh let's say some of us, you may also have other files in that same "Nanas" directory. There may be a file for notes that don't belong anywhere else yet ("Nanas-Nts.docx"), a file of dialogue you haven't yet placed within the script; a file of random plot ideas (you guessed it, "Nanas-Dialogue.docx" and "Nanas-Plot.docx"); and, of course, "Nanas-Outs.docx." (More on "Outs" files in the next chapter.) Pages that you retype during workshops or rehearsals might be named, for example, "R-07-10-June-12" for pages 7 through 10 rewritten on June 12. Etc.

Formatting and presentation:
Keeping organized (and looking good) for your readers

This part is about how to get your script looking professional for when you send it out to people who read them. There are many stage play formats from which you can choose. However, a note, first, on screenwriting:

Screenplay formatting is different. Screenplays are required to have a specific format, used across the industry, so that people who work in film, video, and television can tell at a glance how long a script or a passage is likely to be in screen time. Although the technology is changing, network TV programs must still be timed down to the second. Because screenplay formatting is uniform, an experienced pro can flip through the pages of a screenplay, without

---

67 The ".docx" suffix belongs to Microsoft Word; your suffixes may differ.

even reading the content, and get an accurate idea of how long the show will be.

Playwrights have more leeway. You can open a published stage play, or an unpublished one written by a professional, and find one of a large number of possible formats. But there are some rules that apply to whatever format you choose. (And by the way, writing stage plays in screenplay formatting has long been considered a sign of an inexperienced playwright. Recently it shows signs of growing more popular, but you're still not likely to find many such plays in published form.)

So for your stage play, use a standard, easily readable font, preferably in size 12 type. Larger than size 12 and it looks as though you're trying to make your play look longer than it is; smaller, and it can become difficult to read. Times New Roman 12, the default with Microsoft Word, is probably the most popular. Avoid fancy fonts: an Olde English font, for example, is hard to read and looks as though you're trying to distract the reader from the weak content. And this should hardly need to be said, but black type on a white background!

Most scripts are presented in "portrait" configuration rather than "landscape," on standard letter-sized pages—8½" by 11"—and, if printed on paper, then printed on one side only.

As you can see from *Totally Nana's Ride*, I like the speeches in single space, with double spaces between them. This is pretty standard and is easy to read.

That said, be aware that publishing companies have their own styles, and like to keep the styles of their published volumes consistent for all the plays they put out. So if you submit your play to such a company, be prepared for them to reformat it, or to ask you to reformat it, to match their own style. (For example, the excerpts from plays in this book are in the style used by Scirocco Drama, the stage play imprint of this book's publisher, J. Gordon Shillingford.)

Title and introductory pages

Not everyone does this exactly as described below, but I recommend it: a title page and an "introductory" page, before you then start the play proper on the third page. (I didn't do this in Chapter 6, as *Totally Nana's Ride* is embedded in a longer chapter and having a separate title page would have looked odd and confusing.)

The title page customarily features the title around Line 16, in capitals, in as large a font as you can fit onto one line, followed by "A play by" or "A short play by" and your name, proudly displayed in a somewhat larger font than 12. Then, at the bottom of the page, your contact info.

The "Introductory" page should contain the following:

A list of the characters, or "Dramatis Personae" as they used to call them—ideally without extensive character descriptions, as discussed in Chapter 11.

A description of the setting, again without a lot of detail. In *Totally Nana's Ride*, unconventionally produced as the play was, this called for a slightly longer explanation and a description of the Car itself.

A "Production History," if there is one, including workshops and readings. Again, in *Totally Nana's Ride*, this was a little different. But it should include the names of directors, actors, designers, stage managers, and others who have taken part in important events in the play's history. If it's had a few productions, you need list only the personnel for the original production, but you may want to include participants in a major subsequent production, etc.

"Acknowledgements," where you briefly thank any other people who have contributed to the play's development. This is important! People who have helped you with your script will want to see their names in there, and rightly so.

Now to the stuff at the top of each page: the running heads and page numbers, as mentioned in the above section on "Keeping Organized for Yourself." These features get a bit complicated in Microsoft Word, involving different "sections," and I'm told that they're no less thorny in other programs. So it may take a bit of patient learning, but it pays off in professional appearance and general coolness.

There should be no running head or page number on the title page. The running head first appears on the first introductory page, or pages, and continues through the rest of the script. The page numbers also begin on the first introductory page and continue throughout, but they change. On the introductory page(s), the numbers traditionally read "i, ii, iii," etc., starting with page i, and in the script itself, they turn into the conventional "1, 2, 3," etc., again starting over with page 1. I like to put the page numbers in the top right corner, next to the running head.

Acts and scenes

Most full-length plays are divided into acts, and many acts are divided into scenes. Act headings—"Act One," "Act Two," etc.—are usually placed on a new page, three lines down, with the beginning of the text, or the scene heading, three lines below that. Scene headings within an act can begin on their own new pages, or in mid-page, depending on your mood. The numbering of scenes usually starts over at "Scene One" with each new act, so even if you have three scenes in Act One, your Act Two will begin with "Scene One," not "Scene Four." Don't write the heading "Act One" if it's a one-act play, or "Scene One" if there's only one scene to the act.

Now, as this is about acts and scenes, here are some definitions:

An **act** is a part of the play that begins and/or ends with an **intermission**. And just to be clear, an intermission is a break, with the house lights up and the actors offstage—at least long enough for audience members and actors alike to get to a washroom and/ or grab a drink, and perhaps for the crew to change the set.

The number of acts in conventional plays seems to have dwindled over the last few centuries. Elizabethan plays such as William's were divided into five "acts," but most scholars now believe that there were only one or two actual intermissions, if any. The number has since been steadily reduced until currently it is fashionable to present full-length one-act plays, usually between an hour and 90 minutes long, with no intermission, like most feature films.

A **scene** is a chunk of the play that inhabits a different time and/or place than the scene before and the scene after. Students will sometimes write a scene in which two characters are sitting in the living room having an argument, and then write "Scene Two," and have the same two characters, in the same room, a moment after "Scene One," talking about something else. That's not a new scene. That's a change of subject.

It's very simple: a new scene takes place when you change the *time*, the *place*, or *both*. And there's no ideal number of scenes to have. A play can contain one scene, or a great many, though if you have too many scenes you may run into trouble with set changes or with the audience's attention span.

It's customary to indicate a scene change with a title, "Scene Two," "Scene Three," etc., and a description of the new setting, whether it's separated from the previous one by time, place or both: "The same, a few hours later," "At the same time, in Aunt Helga's parlour," "Next morning in Hedda's bedroom," etc.

However, as with everything else, there are creative exceptions. Not every playwright indicates scene changes in every script. In the first scene of Djanet Sears' *The Adventures of a Black Girl in Search of God* (Toronto: Playwrights Canada Press, 2003), the stage is divided between a church interior during a service and a road, outdoors at night, on which the protagonist is running in the rain; the action switches fluidly back and forth between the two settings, without scene headings to interrupt the flow. In Colleen Murphy's *The Society for the Destitute Presents Titus Bouffonius*, a bouffon adaptation of William's *Titus Andronicus*, the actors take turns simply shouting out each new setting, for example: "The Tomb of the Bouffonii," "A room in the Emperor's palace," "On the plains near Rome," "Outside Titus' house," and "Here we are in a forest where everyone is going to meet up to hunt panthers but fasten your seatbelts because more than a panther will be hunted."[68]

Many plays consist in their entirety of only one scene, especially such short plays as *Totally Nana's Ride* and Edward Albee's *The Zoo Story*. The ancient Greek tragedies were full-length plays

---

68 Colleen Murphy, *The Society for the Destitute Presents Titus Bouffonius* (Winnipeg: Scirocco Drama, 2021).

that consisted of one scene. Indeed, Aristotle proclaimed this to be a virtue, and argued for "unity of time, place and action" as a necessity in the theatre.

There is also a convention, not very common but sometimes seen in farces, where a big moment happens, the lights go to black, there's an intermission, and then Act Two begins at the same moment when the action left off. One might call this one scene in two acts, but of course the resumption would be labelled as "Act Two, Scene One." Examples include Ayckbourn's *Relatively Speaking*, and *What the Butler Saw* (1967) by Joe Orton.

Finally, there's an unusual category called **French scenes**, which you might never use but is a term you should know. Seventeenth-century Parisian playwrights, such as Molière, Racine, and Corneille, indicated scene changes by the entrances and exits of the characters. What we would call the same scene, with a character entering or exiting, was indicated by the Parisian playwrights as a new one, with its own scene number.

The term is almost never used any more, except by stage managers who divide their scripts into them to schedule actors for rehearsals. It is explained here to prepare you for that moment in rehearsal when a director refers to "French scenes" and you want to know what she's talking about.

One more thought about scenes

This last section is about the *content* of scenes. For many years I taught two principles about scenes, and it was not until recently that I realized that they are, in effect, the same principle, articulated in two different ways.

The first principle has already been mentioned, in Chapter 4: that a scene should portray a routine being interrupted. The second principle is that a scene should show at least one of the characters getting something different from what they expected, or else the scene has no reason to exist. It's basically the same principle as the one that a scene is a routine that gets interrupted: the routine is what the characters expect, and the interruption is what they discover instead.

Oddly enough, this appears less true in movies. Movies will frequently devote scenes to showing a character going about their routine business in the course of a normal day. One reason for this difference may be that, as mentioned in Chapter 10, a play happens in a room with live actors presenting a stylized view of things, while watching a film is like looking through a window into something more like reality. Also, changing scenes in a movie requires only an editor's cut, while changing scenes in a play, even one with rapid, fluid staging, requires a little more effort and at least a few seconds more of time—which seems to demand more of a payoff, i.e., a step forward in the plot. And plots do not move forward until characters get something different from what they expect.

13

Finished? Congratulations! Now Write It Again!

Sometimes you have to go a long way out of your way in order to come back a short distance correctly.

—Edward Albee, *The Zoo Story*

Success consists in going from one failure to the next with no loss of enthusiasm.

—Variously attributed to Abraham Lincoln and Winston Churchill

Fall forward.

—Denzel Washington, commencement speech, University of Pennsylvania, May 16, 2011[69]

The top of one mountain is the bottom of the next, so keep climbing.

—André de Shields, Tony Award acceptance speech, 2019[70]

---

69 https://www.rev.com/blog/transcripts/denzel-washington-fall-forward-commencement-speech-transcript

70 https://www.hollywoodreporter.com/video/andr-de-shields-wins-tony-award-hadestown-watch-1216940/

So you've finished your first draft! Congratulations! Now don't read it over! Just send it out to the theatres as is, and soon the praise, contracts, advance cheques, cast lists, and production schedules will be pouring in! Right? Yeah, no, just messing with your head here.

In reality, a painful moment familiar to artists is that feeling of finally knowing you got it right and handing it over to someone whose opinion you respect, only to be told tactfully that it still needs a lot more work. Of course, it's worse when you *don't* get that good advice, and don't do that extra work, and your play is rushed onstage prematurely, resulting in empty houses, bad reviews, and guilt over your actor friends' having to go through this every night.

If you're a beginner, you might as well know sooner than later that this experience doesn't go away. You never outgrow the childish desire for *this* draft to be the one that knocks their socks off, or the disappointment when they tell you it's not ready yet.

So get used to it now. Clock how much time after they tell you to rewrite your play that you spend lying on the bed feeling sorry for yourself and quitting playwriting forever before you get up and go back to the script. At the beginning of my career it was a week or so. With many years of hard experience, I've got it down to a few hours.

Shut up and keep rewriting

It may be wise to resist the impulse to show your finished first draft to too many people. In fact, throughout that early, solitary stage, it may be best not even to tell too many people what it's *about*. For one thing, talking a lot about a writing project can take the energy out of it. Some of your internal drive to write the play is a desire to tell that story, and if you keep telling the story, you'll have less emotional reason to write the play. This is not to suggest you be secretive about it: if people ask, you can tell them! It's just that it can deplete your storytelling energy if you go babbling it around too much.

For another thing, there seem always to be people around who think it's their job to discourage you. A friend of mine asked Stephen Sondheim what he was working on. Sondheim said he no longer talked about his projects, ever since the 1970s when he had told people he was writing a musical about a barber who slit people's throats and whose girlfriend then ground up the murder victims, baked them into meat pies, and sold them to the public. Everybody had told him it would never get produced. It was, of course, *Sweeney Todd*, one of the most successful musicals ever written.

But do keep rewriting. Read it over, frequently. Mutter the dialogue under your breath, or speak it out nice and loud if nobody else is home. Feel the dialogue in your mouth. "Carry around" a line or a passage with you, ruminating on it, as advised in the sections of Chapter 8 on "Rhythm" and on "Chewability and inkfish."

When we listen to early takes of famous pop songs, see early versions of iconic scenes from movies, or read early drafts of renowned pieces of writing, it's sometimes startling to discover how blindly the artists groped towards their masterpieces. A striking recent example appears in the Peter Jackson documentary *Get Back* (Apple Corps Ltd., 2021), with Paul McCartney struggling and fumbling in the direction of what was to become the smash hit title song, while Ringo looks bored and George yawns.

When we see or hear such early efforts, we think, "Didn't *they* know how this famous work goes? Everybody *else* knows how this famous work goes!" But no, what we know is the result of their struggles. They had to try everything else first, and so do the rest of us.

Hollywood screenwriter David Milch produced and wrote a TV series called *Deadwood* in the early 2000s. Part of the supporting material for the series DVDs is a short video about how Milch worked, which included dictating his dialogue aloud to a typist, and repeating it obsessively with variations as he thought of rewrites and changes. One of the actors, W. Earl Brown, says:

> I decided to time him once. It was a two-and-one-third-page scene. He spent five hours rewriting that scene. I swear, he would change a sentence twenty or thirty times. He distills the language down to its most potent form, 'cause it's like he

takes a big chunk of coal—bunch of words that are a chunk
of coal—and you just keep pressin' 'em and pressin' 'em until
they become that—diamond of dialogue. [71]

It's a lovely image, and I mean no disrespect to that fine actor and
perceptive fellow W. Earl Brown, but a playwright hearing that
might feel the way most actors feel when non-actors marvel over
their ability to learn all those lines and say them as if they really
mean them. Because, although Milch does it more obsessively and
better than most of us, *that's the job*: pressing big, dirty hunks of
verbiage down into diamonds of dialogue. And you do it by going
over the dialogue, over and over—and largely by cutting.

Cutting

How do you carve a statue of an elephant? Take a block of
marble and chop off everything that doesn't look like an
elephant.

—Old joke

Cutting is the commonest and most useful technique in rewriting.
Look for places to tighten the script and abbreviate. Look for over-
explanations, repeated info, subtext on the surface—the words "I'm
going to," which could be replaced with "I'll"—and so forth. As the
American playwright David Mamet says, "the only thing we, as
audience, care about in the theater is WHAT HAPPENS NEXT?"[72]

Kill your darlings. That indispensable piece of advice has been
attributed to Eudora Welty, G.K. Chesterton, William Faulkner,
Oscar Wilde, Arthur Quiller-Couch, and others, and it's the title
of a 2013 movie about the Beat poets. The rule has its exceptions,
but any dialogue that's in there to show the audience what a good

---

71 *Deadwood* DVD, Season 2, Episodes 11-12, supporting material: *Trusting
the Process*. This material includes a scene of Milch dictating his dialogue: the
only footage I've ever seen that actually shows a writer writing, and out loud.
Warning for extremely coarse language.

72 David Mamet, "A Playwright in Hollywood," *Writing in Restaurants* (New
York: Penguin Books, 1986), 76.

writer you are should be cut first, as advised in the section "Control Your Cleverness" in Chapter 8.

Mamet rephrases the rule "Kill your darlings" as follows:

> If the action of a character in one scene, for example, is to FLEE THE COUNTRY, we know that a good way to start would be by having him LEAVE THE ROOM. But most of us are loath to eliminate the moving "Death of my Kitten" speech the hero utters on his exit.

The necessary progression is:

> TANIA: Franz, the Army of the Reds is in the Village Square, and you must leave.
>
> FRANZ: See you in Bucharest. *(He exits.)*

But we lie to ourselves, hoping that no one will notice the interruption of the action, and the scene is written:

> TANIA: Franz, the Army of the Reds is in the Village Square, and you must leave.
>
> FRANZ: Leave? Leave? How *many* ways there are to leave! When I was young I had a kitten… (etc.)[73]

So there you have it. Kill your dead kittens. Cutting isn't just a matter of trimming the edges. You're not really cutting unless it hurts: unless you cut to the heart and soul, to the bone. You want to cut good stuff: stuff you just know the audience would have loved. My friends and I have often come out of the theatre after seeing a new play and agreed that inside that mediocre two-hour play was a really good hour-and-fifteen-minute play trying to get out. How you let it out is by cutting the other forty-five. Maybe those deleted minutes will have their own play some day.

Never feel bad about cutting. Nothing you cut has been wasted. Every cut is a gift to the audience. They don't know what they're missing. Cutting, like weeding a garden, is an act of creativity, not destruction. Cutting is a way of liberating the uncut stuff. My mother used to draw with her pencil in one hand and an eraser in

---

73 *Writing in Restaurants*. The "(etc.)" at the end is Mamet's, not mine.

the other and looked just as happy while plying the eraser as the pencil.

Nor should you regret the time spent on that passage you're cutting. Every piece of writing that you cut has helped you get to the stuff you don't cut. The stuff you cut bleeds helpfully into the stuff you keep, sometimes in ways you may not consciously be aware of.

One useful way to approach this is to overwrite deliberately (though within reason), putting in everything that occurs to you, and then cut mercilessly later. In other words, first you put in everything you can, then you take out everything you can, and whatever's left is the play. Sometimes you find yourself both cutting old material and adding new material at the same time, or in rapid alteration. It's a little like preparing a reduction sauce: throwing in new ingredients while boiling off the excess. Done right, it makes the results thicker and richer.

As mentioned previously, have a file called "Outs" in your play directory. If you cut anything you might theoretically want back in future, copy it into the "Outs" file. Your "Outs" file may wind up as long as the play. (The "Outs" file for this book is almost as long as the book, which means that the book could have been almost twice as long as it is. You're welcome.) Of course, most or all of that "Outs" material will remain unused; but whenever you want something back that you've cut—and it does happen—you'll know where to find it.

There is much to be said for spending *time* on rewriting (that is, if you're not on a deadline). There are exceptions—some great plays have been written in short periods of time—but it normally takes from months to a couple of years to finish a full-length play. Beware of books and courses that will teach you to write that play, novel or screenplay in *just a few painless weeks*! By spending time on your rewrites, you get to know your characters better. It's gratifying to live with them long enough to begin to know what they'll do in any situation.

That's one of the reasons not to feel bad over the stuff you cut: it has taught you more about your characters. Even the time you spend away from the play can be productive. You may find, when you return to it, that some work got done while it was sitting in your subconscious mind. Sometimes, problems that seemed intractable have solved themselves in the interim, without your conscious effort. (Admittedly, sometimes they've got worse. That's life. I didn't write this book to lie to you.)

Don't be embarrassed by your previous drafts. We playwrights have an advantage over actors: when actors are criticized, it is their actual bodies, faces, and voices under attack. But we playwrights have this convenient paper prop we carry around in our hands, so that we can point to passages we no longer like, and say, "Oh, that bit? I wrote that yesterday, when I was young and stupid."

The solo workshop

Some years ago, I came up with what I call the **solo workshop**, which is a technique to apply at almost the last stage of rewriting before showing your script to somebody else, and which replicates a group workshop. The **group workshop** is, briefly, a gathering of playwright, director, actors, and sometimes a stage manager, to read a play-in-progress out loud and offer the playwright feedback for improvements. It will be described in detail in the next chapter. The solo workshop is a group workshop you do by yourself.

As with the "There's This Nurse" exercise, begin with the character you've paid the least attention to: the smallest role, or the character with the fewest lines. Reread that character's scenes as if you were the actor playing that character.

Ask yourself the questions actors ask: Where is my character coming from when I enter? Where is she going when I exit? What is she doing while offstage? When onstage, what's she thinking about while the others are talking, what are her motivations, and what does she want at every given moment? Try to ignore the other stuff: the plot, theme, other characters. All you care about right now is what this character is going through while she's thinking that this play is real life.

You'll find mistakes—some subtle and some painfully obvious, some tiny and some that might force you to rethink the whole thing. You may find that, as you rewrite this character's dialogue, you must rewrite other characters' responses to it. So write those changes, or make a note to yourself to write them later.

And then, when you've finished with that character, move on to the one you've paid the second-least amount of attention to, and do it again. Keep doing that, once for each character, up to the lead characters whom you've been paying the most attention to anyway.

Vancouver's Electric Company Theatre, who often devise their scripts as a group, came up with an improvement on this technique. They use the solo workshop to investigate each character but have added one more "character" to the mix: the audience. They go through the draft one more time, thinking about what the viewers know, or think they know, or wonder about because they don't know. It's an invaluable addition.

Drafts, passes, and technology

The next chapter, and Part Four of the book, begins with your showing a draft to somebody else, so it's time to define **drafts**.

The meaning of the word has changed with the advent of computers. In the era of typewriters, you scribbled in longhand on the most recent draft (typed on paper, of course), until you could barely read it any more, or until somebody else—theatre company, agent, teacher—needed to read what you had so far. Then you typed the whole thing over again, numbered that as the new draft, sent a copy to the person who wanted to read it, and started scribbling on the carbon copy you kept, towards the *next* draft.

These days, with little or no scribbling, the definition of "draft" has changed, and you call your work a completed draft because it's time to print it out or e-mail it, to show to somebody else; and Microsoft Word and other programs offer "markup" features, so that dramaturges and editors can insert their notes into your document.

Or, sometimes, you start a fresh draft for yourself, if you have a new idea for a radical reworking of your play but want to keep what you've got so far in case the new idea doesn't work or requires lots of the old stuff blended into it.

In any case, there are now fewer "drafts" per play than there used to be. I use the word "pass" to describe the process that used to be more of a "draft": a reading-through and rewriting of the script, sometimes with one specific purpose in mind or problem to look for and solve.

There may still be occasions when you'll want to print out a passage, or the whole thing, scribble on it with pen and ink, and then type up the scribbles. It feels good to turn those paper pages; it's also the best way to look at two versions of a passage and compare them.

Students sometimes ask how many drafts it takes to get a play to a producible level. They do understand that there's no hard and fast answer; they just want a ballpark figure. So: some of my one-acts took only two or three drafts; the largest number of drafts I have recorded for one (full-length) play is 14. Ordinarily the number tends to hover between four and eight. But, of course, it's different for every playwright.

When you're ready to show it to others

When you've finished your solo workshop and then made the resultant changes—or simply got the draft to the point where you don't know what to do with it next—that's the time to show it to somebody, or somebodies, else, and get their opinions.

One of the pleasures of this art form is that it's both solitary and collaborative. You work in a sort of expanding world. You start out writing in solitude. When it's going well, you feel like you have this cool secret which you will soon unleash upon an unsuspecting public. Then you work with perhaps one dramaturge, then with a small group—maybe in a workshop situation—then with the larger group that consists of cast and crew, and finally with the audience.

We're now ready to move on—from the topic of developing your script on your own to the topic of developing your script with the help of others. This calls for a new chapter and a new section of the book.

PART 4

HOW TO WORK AND PLAY WELL WITH OTHERS

14

Dramaturges, Workshops, and Readings

Showing it to others

The next chapters are about how to show your play to others, get notes from them, and rewrite on the basis of those notes, without messing up your play, making enemies, or both. There are five stages of developing your play with the aid of other people. This chapter is about the first three—individual dramaturges, group workshops, and readings—and later chapters are about the final two: rehearsal and performance. [74]

Start by finding yourself a **dramaturge**, or **dramaturg**. The word has two spellings because it has two meanings. A dramaturg in the traditional European sense, usually spelled without the E, is a literary manager for a theatre company, who helps choose plays, researches their backgrounds, consults with the playwrights, writes program notes, contributes to the publicity work, etc. The

---

74 A colleague who was giving me editorial help on this book read an earlier draft of this chapter, in which this first paragraph was not yet very clear, and called out to me from a different room, "What are the five stages?" Not realizing she was talking about the book, I replied with Dr. Elisabeth Kübler-Ross' five stages of learning that you're dying—"Denial, anger, bargaining, depression, and acceptance"—which is also not a bad description of the rewriting process.

other meaning, used here, with the E, is a personal one-to-one script editor who helps you with your play.

If you're writing the play as part of a class or a writers' group, the decision is made for you. Otherwise you might start by writing up a list of the people whose opinions you'd take seriously. This is no time for nepotism. Your parents, siblings, best buddy since kindergarten, or boyfriend / girlfriend / partner will see it when it opens. Right now, you need people whose opinions you will respect even if they hurt: a teacher, colleague, director, actor, etc. (Of course, if your parents, girlfriend, etc. are also experienced theatre artists, you can ask, but, again, be prepared for serious criticism—or fallout in other areas of your life!)

When you ask, ask nicely. Don't take your reader's skills and expertise for granted: giving tactful but useful notes on a script is hard work. Unless your reader is being paid by a theatre or script development centre, or offers their services for free, offer something in return. If you have money, the going rate in 2023 is one or two hundred dollars for your reader's time. If you don't have money, offer to mow their lawn, babysit their kid, etc. And unless it's otherwise agreed on in advance, you're asking for their comments on only one draft: don't keep sending them rewrites.

How to receive notes

When you begin to get that critique you asked for—whether it's from an individual dramaturge, or, later, a whole bunch of actors and a director ganging up on you in a workshop or rehearsal— it's almost a certainty that some of it will hurt. So take it like a grownup. Assume your reader is trying to do this as accurately but kindly as possible. (That's assuming you've chosen your reader well. If their feedback seems unkind, useless, or both, first take some time to make sure there's nothing you can get out of it, and then, if it really is futile, blame yourself for choosing your reader badly.) In any case, don't get sullen. Even if you're paying for it with money or return favours, what you're getting is a gift.

The way it works is that your dramaturge—or, later, everybody in the workshop—reads and/or listens to your play; perhaps reads or hears your account of what you're trying to do with it; forms their own *inevitably distorted, inaccurate* ideas of what you want to do; and gives you feedback based on those distorted and inaccurate images—in other words, based on how brilliant the play would be if they wrote it themselves.

They do this in good faith and with good will. It's the only way to do it. It's what you will do, too, when you read somebody else's play or take part in their workshop. But when you're the playwright, your job is to sift your way through their distorted, inaccurate images, and find the stuff that could actually help your play—in other words, to decide what notes to take and what notes to leave aside.

The notes they give you will vary in size. Some will be small, simple pointers that immediately strike you as accurate and easy to implement, and others will offer painful, complicated truths that go to the heart of your play and make you want to throw the whole thing out. It may seem logical to start with the big, complicated, difficult notes, and save the small, simple stuff for later, but this is backwards: both inefficient and disheartening. Instead, start with your reader's simplest suggestions: they will boost your morale, and clear out some of the underbrush so that you can see the larger, more complicated notes more clearly.

Don't be ashamed not to understand a note, but politely ask the reader to explain it again. Try not to be defensive, but just listen. And don't be ashamed to disagree with a note, but make sure you really understand it before you disagree aloud.

The process can be demoralizing: often, your dramaturge, or everybody else in the room, seems to understand your play better than you do. If it's a group, everything one person says contradicts something somebody else says. If it's a single dramaturge, half of what they say contradicts something else they just said. They tell you to add stuff and make it shorter; to keep it funny and make it serious; and so on. Relax. Breathe.

Some playwrights think everybody else actually *does* understand their play better than they do, so they sway with every wind that blows, and take every single note offered. That was me, before I learned better. This may be out of fear of missing an opportunity, or fear of offending people by not taking their notes. But they do, or should, understand that not all their notes will be accepted, or will work.

Other playwrights do the opposite. One actor friend, taking part in a workshop of another friend's new play, said in frustration, "He's not workshopping the play; he just sits there and defends it." This too is a result of fear—of losing what we've already achieved by rewriting some good stuff out of existence—or perhaps the fear that if we accept too many notes from others, the play will not be ours any more. This last one is silly: we're there precisely to "steal" from each other, and dramaturges and workshop participants understand that too. Part of the purpose of the "Acknowledgements" paragraph in the script, described in Chapter 12, is to compensate people for their "stolen" ideas.

And that acknowledgement, besides any previously-agreed-upon money, return favours, etc., is the only further compensation you owe them. In the standard contracts negotiated by the Playwrights Guild of Canada and the Professional Association of Canadian Theatres, or PACT, there is a clause that says, "No changes shall be made in the script without the consent of the Playwright. All changes become the sole property of the Playwright." It's the second sentence that concerns us here. If an actor suggests a line and you put it in, they can't then demand a percentage of your royalties. On the other hand, don't ask them to improvise large swatches of dialogue which you will then insert into your play without their permission.

Working your notes into the draft

During workshops and rehearsals, you'll be sitting there taking notes. Some notes may apply to a specific moment in the play— "Trim this speech"—and some affect everything: "Give everybody a Scottish accent." It's best to type those immediate rehearsal notes into their own separate file with a filename including the date (or, of course, scribble them into your notebook). Later, you can copy and paste those notes into the front of your current draft. Still later, when you have the time, copy each specific note, still in note form, into the place in the script where it belongs. And those general

"Scottish-accent" notes that affect the whole play can continue to live at the beginning of the script, until you've incorporated them throughout.

When you're doing rewrites based on your notes, you'll probably start at the beginning and work toward the end, but there's no rule saying you must. Sometimes you can jump ahead to a note that other notes depend on, and fix that problem first, which lends a kind of ease to doing the rest.

Proofreading

You may or may not be gifted with an eye that catches mistakes in spelling, punctuation, and grammar. Having one seems to be like having an ear for music or a sense of colour: it can be improved with training, but basically, it seems some of us have it or learn it in childhood, and some of us don't. Being able to spot such errors isn't necessarily a sign of intelligence, and not being good at it doesn't mean you're not a good writer. But if your script is riddled with typos and other small mistakes, it may make the work look less professional than you'd like.

So if you're not one of those lucky folks who have errors jumping off the screen to greet them, then first of all, use your spell-checking and grammar-checking programs. But as we all know, they don't catch everything. So follow up by finding somebody who's good at this, and willing to look over your script before you send it out. Proofreading is a different skill from dramaturgy, but you might want to request assistance in the same way: offer them a few bucks or a return favour. And a dramaturge who is also a good proofreader is worth their weight in rubies.

Script development centres

Back on the general subject of dramaturgy: playwrights enjoy helping each other, and have formed organizations for that purpose, called script development centres or playwrights' centres, which can be found in most of Canada's larger cities. These groups help playwrights develop specific plays, and offer such other services as advocacy, networking, and events like public staged readings and classes. They also sometimes link up with theatre companies for joint productions of plays they've helped develop.

These centres offer dramaturges, usually experienced playwrights themselves, who will read your new play in development and give you a written or face-to-face critique, sometimes at a small charge and sometimes for free if you're a member. Often the one-on-one critique is the first in a graduated series of steps, continuing with script workshops, public readings, and maybe full productions.

There is also a national umbrella organization called the Playwrights Guild of Canada, which we'll look at in Chapter 16, "The Biz." And American, British, and other readers will find equivalent organizations in their own countries.

Roughly speaking, there's one of these centres per province in Canada, and each one works for the playwrights from all over its province. They keep their membership fees low, and lower for students. If you're serious about playwriting, I couldn't advise you more strongly to join one of these groups. Besides getting help with your own play, there's entertainment and educational value in attending other playwrights' workshops and readings. You might also be surprised to discover how good playwrights are at partying. And nobody will look down on you if you're not an experienced playwright. These people know that their members come from all levels of interest and experience, and they welcome newcomers to the art form.

Workshops and rehearsals: a comparison

After you've looked at your play one-on-one with a dramaturge, taken their notes and done a rewrite, you might be ready to graduate to a group **workshop**. This activity, under one name or another, is probably as old as theatre itself. Just about every major playwright in history has been closely associated with a working theatre, and they weren't there just for the beer. There's no doubt that they were there to hear their drafts read aloud by actors while the play was in progress.

Workshops and early rehearsals look alike. If you walk into a rehearsal room during one or the other, you'll find everybody sitting around a table, reading the lines and discussing them. You might not be able to tell at first whether these people are workshopping a new play, or in early rehearsal—the **table work**—for a full production. But the purposes are different.

The purpose of *rehearsals* is to get this pre-existing script to make sense by opening night, without changing too much of the text. Of course, that's standard practice when the playwright is dead or unavailable. If she's alive, available, and willing to rewrite, especially if it's a first production, the cast may request script changes, but that's not the main purpose of rehearsals. And significant rewrites by directors and actors *without* the playwright's knowledge are illegal (see that contract clause quoted above) and frowned upon even when the work is in the public domain, though small cuts and changes can be gotten away with.

On the other hand, the entire purpose of a *workshop* is to help the playwright rewrite. When actors in a workshop find moments that don't work for them, their job is to point them out to the playwright and explain the problem they're having, rather than finding ways to finesse the existing dialogue into making more sense, as they do in rehearsal.

The workshop in more detail

The workshop is a blessing and a godsend and a fundamental tool for making your play better. It is invaluable to have real live fellow artists who are willing to go bravely into your freshly built or half-built structure for you; to look out at the play from the inside, through the eyes of individual characters; and to come back out and report to you on what they found there. They represent your characters and speak for them. The great American trumpeter Wynton Marsalis said, "The real power of jazz [...] is that a group of people can come together and [...] negotiate their agendas with each other. And that negotiation is the art."[75] Playwriting can also be described as a group of people negotiating their agendas,

75 *Jazz*, a documentary mini-series by Ken Burns, Florentine Films, Episode 1.

184 TWO WAYS ABOUT IT

with the difference that all the people except the playwright are imaginary. In a workshop, those imaginary people suddenly have real, flesh-and-blood humans to negotiate their agendas on their behalf.

Actors in a workshop are useful not as literary critics, but *as actors*. In *Text and Context*, Richard Greenblatt puts it very well:

> Even if the actor is a writer or a dramaturg themselves (or perhaps especially if they are), the feedback that is most helpful to the writer is from an actor's point of view. The actor's perspective is, by definition, far more subjective and focused on their character, and not on the whole. It is far more valuable to the writer for an actor to say, "I'm confused as to why I suddenly lash out here," than to say, "Lashing out is a poor dramaturgical choice." The input needed from actors is "actor-ish." [...] After all, it is the actor who has to decipher, explore, interpret and ultimately perform these words. To find out what is clear and what isn't, what feels "playable" and what doesn't, and how the story of each character feels to the actor, can be wonderfully useful. In a sense, the actor becomes the advocate for their character.[76]

Workshops can take different forms and have different rules. One director I know routinely demands that the actors never make statements to the playwright, but only ask questions of her, which she must not respond to at the time, but must take away and think about. (And "Wouldn't it be cool if you changed it so that [etc.]?" is not considered a question.) Greenblatt will follow a workshop with written questions for the actors, such as, "Three questions you have about your character," "Three things you like about the play," "What is the play about (in twenty-five words or less)," etc.[77]

Many workshops are scheduled to allow for rewrite time, so that the playwright can go home, or into the next room; have a good cry; pound out a few rewritten pages; and bring the new pages back to hear them aloud. Greenblatt categorizes his workshops

---

76 *Text and Context*, 170.

77 *Text and Context*, 173.

as "Half-Day or One-Day Workshops" and "Three-to-Six-Day Workshops."[78] Also, you may wind up writing a draft or two, or more, between a workshop and the play's first rehearsals; and a play in development might have more than one workshop.

Don't direct your own workshop. (As a general rule, playwrights shouldn't direct their own productions either; I'll get to why, later.) If you can't find a director for your workshop, you may be better off postponing it until you do. You need a director to run things, to provide a different viewpoint on the work, and to provoke or muzzle you as appropriate.

You'd also be well advised not to take any of the acting roles, not to be the one who reads the stage directions aloud—and, indeed, not even to read along silently in your script while the actors perform the dialogue. You've been using your eyes while writing the thing so far; now it's time to use your ears.

Workshops can reveal a lot about your play's structure. We are called "wrights" because, like cartwrights, wheelwrights and wainwrights ("wain" being a barrel or keg), we *construct* our product.[79] And the actors are the ones who will have to live inside that construction, at least for a time.

Workshops at home: pizza, beer, etc.

If you happen not to live in a city big enough to support professional theatres or a script development organization, or if there are such companies but for some reason nobody else wants to help you with a workshop, there's no reason not to do one yourself.

Make it a party. Provide pizza, soft drinks, and perhaps beer or equivalent.[80] (The food can be served before the actual reading and discussion, but the beer or equivalent should wait until after the reading and most of the discussion. Can you guess why?)

---

78 *Text and Context*, 172–176.

79 Perhaps confusingly, though we are playwrights, our activity is spelled "playwriting."

80 Must be of legal age. Suggestion void where prohibited by law.

Professionals usually expect to be paid for their time; but students and amateur actors (and, sometimes, professionals too) will often be happy with a cheap dinner, a beer and/or a toke—and, of course, that all-important mention under "Acknowledgements" in future drafts, programs, and publications of the play. This is not exploitative of the actors, as long as everybody knows in advance what the deal is.

Choose actors and a director whose judgment you trust. (It's generally understood that inviting actors and a director to be in your workshop does not oblige you to make sure they'll wind up in the production.) You may or may not have the luxury of a stage manager, but you may not need one, as long as you're willing to do the grunt work of providing the copies of the script, the refreshments, etc., yourself. But, as mentioned above, do ask a director to oversee the proceedings; and go over the script with her in advance. Get the scripts to all the actors in advance as well.

You might want to invite a few more people to serve as a small audience. Those people need not be theatre experts. There's nothing wrong with having some normal humans there to represent your future audience, so this is where the parents, siblings, and boyfriends come in. Your roommate's cousin, who's never been in a theatre in her life, may ask you a question that will open up the entire play for you.

Finally, don't be distracted by the pizza, etc. into thinking this is merely a party for the purpose of celebrating your genius. It should still be an opportunity for constructive criticism and serious work. Some playwrights and directors provide workshop participants and listeners with postcards or an e-mail address so that they can send comments later. This can make for more honest responses. Sometimes questions are provided: Was anything unclear? Was anything *too* clear? What would you have liked more of? Less of? How would you sum up the play? Etc.

Hearing your lines for the first time: a study in pain

Workshops and rehearsals both begin with read-throughs. Usually, the director welcomes everyone; you the playwright might say a few words; if it's a rehearsal, designers and other specialists may show off their designs; and then the read-through begins—you put your script aside and listen, instead of reading along, because I told you to—and from the first moment, it's as wrong as wrong can be.

Guaranteed: it'll be too fast or too slow, too loud or too quiet, too angry or too happy, too sad, too funny or not funny enough. They'll emphasize the wrong word in the sentence, the wrong sentence in the speech, the wrong speech in the scene. They will misunderstand entire sections. And as you hear your beloved dialogue being mangled and ruined, you know what you must do? You must do nothing but breathe deeply and listen.

Do not speak. Do not grunt or moan in pain. Do not give non-verbal cues: no rolling your eyes, squirming in your chair, scribbling ostentatiously in your notebook, typing loudly on your laptop, or trying to exchange meaningful looks with your director, who, if they're any good, will not look back at you, because they'll be busy doing what you should be doing: listening carefully to, and learning a lot from, exactly how the actors are wrecking your dialogue.

You can glean much information from remaining silent and listening to that first read-through. They may be doing it perfectly well, but just not in a way that you ever imagined. It's a very common experience to think, "That's completely wrong, that's not how I—Oh, wait a second, that's really interesting." And even when a line reading is really and truly wrong, you can learn a lot from how, and why, they're doing it wrong.

They'll also read some of it "right," i.e., just as you intended it, and it may still be terrible, and that'll be *your* fault. Lines that were deathless prose when you wrote them will now be clunky and awkward. You'll even become aware of how bad some of your lines are, two or three speeches *before* the actors speak them, but, tempted as you may be to call for a sudden break or insert a new intermission on the spot, you really can't do anything to forestall the humiliation. You'll marvel that you didn't spot these problems before, no matter how much rewriting you've done, solo workshops and all. Parts will be too long or too brief; not clear enough or too clear; active but unmotivated, or motivated but inactive; containing the same word twice in the same sentence, containing the letter "B" too often within the same line, and so on.

But at other times, the actors will say lovely, surprising things that you'll remember you invented, and the line you weren't sure was funny will get a big laugh, and an actor will make a line sound better than you realized, and for a moment the world will be a bright and shining place. All in all, it's a roller-coaster of an experience—as theatre should be.

Why is this? Why do problems you've never noticed before become crystal-clear as soon as you hear the text spoken aloud by somebody else? Perhaps it's that difference in perception between your eyes and your ears. Perhaps it's because you're dealing with three different rates of speed: your thinking speed, your handwriting or typing speed, and the speed at which the words are spoken. Or perhaps there's just that magical unknown factor that the actors, bless them, bring to the process. But all this takes place before we add the next, and most unpredictable, factor: the audience.

Readings

Often the first time a play meets an audience is in the form of a staged reading, when it is still a work in progress. Like the workshop, the staged reading is a frequent tool in play development. Professionals spend at least as much time, if not more, attending staged readings as we do at full productions. And like workshops, staged readings have different styles. Some are public, and some are just for invited audiences of friends, family and/or experts.

Usually readings are free of charge, but the audience earns their entertainment by staying in their seats afterwards and offering their opinions to the playwright. Sometimes there are printed programs, and sometimes questionnaires for audience members to answer.

Customarily, the actors sit onstage with their scripts, often with music stands or similar lecterns. The director hosts the event, welcoming the audience and introducing the playwright, stage manager, and actors. During the reading itself, the director reads the stage directions, and the playwright sits in the audience, makes notes, and suffers.

There is a spectrum of styles of presentation. At one end is the commonest approach: the actors in a scene simply stand up to read while the others remain seated. But sometimes passages are blocked in advance and performed on their feet, and sometimes there are costume pieces, props, and theatrical devices. Indeed, some staged readings look almost like full productions, but with the actors **on book**, which means still holding their scripts because they haven't learned their lines. (Obviously, **off book** means free of their scripts because they've learned them.)

As you did when you first heard the lines aloud, you will see the play differently at a staged reading for an audience. It can be painful or exhilarating, and either way you can learn a lot. Your perception of the whole play is altered just by the presence of fresh eyes and ears in the room. You become intently aware of when they laugh and when they don't; when they seem restless and when there's the wonderful deep silence of an audience thinking and feeling together; when a moment works as expected, works differently, or doesn't work at all.

After the reading, the playwright usually joins the cast onstage for a talk with the audience. Many audience members are not experienced theatre people, but, as with the roommate's cousin who asked the great question in your workshop, don't assume that their input will not be of use. They almost always include savvy individuals with interesting ideas. They also, after all, represent the public who, you hope, will someday buy tickets for this; so listen to everybody.

Seeking production: simply sending it out there

How do you actually get your show onto a stage? If your play has had workshops and/or readings, then by the time it's ready to consider for production, it may have had some exposure to people who can produce it. A script development centre might promote it to a local company, or you might have developed the script *within* such a company, who are now willing or eager to get it onto their stage. Those occasions are, of course, delightful. However, let's assume it's your job to get your play out there by yourself. Let's start with the simplest approach: sending it out to the theatres.

You might ask around for yourself, to find out which theatres prefer you to submit your play by regular mail, and which as an e-mail attachment. One artistic director, a friend who I hoped was kidding, said, "Send it both ways, so I can ignore both of them."

If you're sending it electronically, copy it as a .PDF, or other un-editable format, so that nobody can accidentally (or, Heaven forbid, purposefully) change your text. The filename need not match the title exactly—often it's a shortened version of the title—but should consist of a word or two identifying the title unmistakably, followed by a hyphen or underscore, followed by your last name, as: "Nanas_Lazarus.pdf." Dramaturges and editors have many scripts to deal with, so identifying yours clearly makes their job easier—and makes them likelier to look upon your play with favour!

If you're sending it on paper, have it bound—three holes with brads will do, but so will the plastic spiral binding provided by copying services—and give it a front and back in cover stock, with the title and your name on the front.

In either case, include a short and sweet cover letter, brief and to the point. Make it clear that you're submitting it for them to consider producing on their stage. There's nothing wrong with, "I attach my new play, *Bob the Blob Loblaw*, which I am submitting for your consideration for production. I hope you like it. Sincerely," etc. Don't explain at length who you are and how you came to write the play, and *certainly* don't explain how great it is and how stupid they would be to reject it. You can put more details about the play and its development on the Introductory page of the script itself. But also make sure your name and contact info are in both the cover letter and the script.

Canadian theatres, sad to say, don't have a great reputation for responding promptly. In their defence, their collections of unsolicited scripts often grow very large, and they don't usually have a big budget for readers. So, to help them out with their task of reading all our uncalled-for stuff, know your theatre! Make sure the script you're sending is appropriate for them. It's astonishing how often theatres receive scripts from playwrights who've never checked the theatres' mandates—especially nowadays, when checking usually consists simply in visiting their websites. There's no excuse for sending your hot new sex farce satirizing the BDSM crowd to a TYA theatre, or, conversely, sending your children's fairy tale to a cutting-edge-late-night-queer-ironic-retro-nerdlesque company. And if you live in the same community as a theatre you're submitting to, then for Heaven's sake, go see their shows!

Seeking production: Fringes and other festivals

If your play is appropriate to the Fringe format—i.e., a small cast, inexpensive production values and a running time of about 45 minutes—consider producing it yourself with friends and staging it at a Fringe or a juried festival.

The Fringe Festival is a proud Canadian invention. Around 1982, Edmonton theatre director Brian Paisley attended the Edinburgh Festival and its associated Fringe Festival, and came home from Scotland with a brilliant idea: why not just put on a local Fringe festival, without bothering with a mainstream festival for it to be attached to? And thus was born the Edmonton Fringe—and the Vancouver Fringe, Winnipeg Fringe, Toronto Fringe, and all the others.

Current Fringes take place in both conventional theatre spaces and in churches, schools, storefronts, and sometimes weirder venues. Traditionally, the shows are under an hour long. Interestingly, Fringes are *not juried*: nobody chooses or rejects the shows. The applications are pulled at random out of a barrel, often literally, at a party where the lucky applicants drink and dance with the unlucky ones.

For ambitious theatre artists, the fact that the Fringes are not juried is a gift. You don't have to jump through the hoops of presenting a proposal to a jury, or worry that the deck might be somehow stacked against you. So the Fringes have become showcases for beginning artists eager to establish their names, and for seasoned pros who use them to produce work that they can't do elsewhere.

You compile your own team of director, designer(s), actor(s) and producer(s), which gives you complete creative freedom, as well as the experience of producing a show from the ground up. The Fringes make a serious, honourable attempt to keep ticket prices low, and have an admirable policy of making sure that all the box office revenue goes to the artists.

There are also juried festivals, such as Toronto's annual SummerWorks, which specializes in new plays, offering performances of both finished works and works in progress. You must submit a script[81] and a description of the proposed production to get into those juried festivals. Of course, the juries often say no, even to good work, when the number of promising applications exceeds the number of available slots. But because of this, getting produced at a juried festival provides a cachet that the Fringes cannot provide. There's also more leeway in terms of performance duration.

Seeking production: competitions

Playwriting competitions also provide a way to get your new play noticed. For one example, the Playwrights Guild's Tom Hendry Awards are an annual set of contests in various categories, including drama, comedy, musical theatre, and theatre for young audiences. Interestingly, in some categories, it is a requirement that the play *not* be previously produced.

Some other play competitions are run by universities, such as the Voaden Prize, administered by Queen's University and named after early Canadian playwright Herman Voaden, and open to all Canadian citizens or landed immigrants. And some contests are run by theatre companies, professional and amateur.

I used to be opposed to competitions in the arts—partly because my politics generally lean to the left, and partly because in the arts (unlike in athletics, where competitions make sense), everyone is going after a unique "personal best," and the achievement cannot be measured in numbers for comparison purposes. But over the years, I've modified my position. Once I started attending awards

---

81   Non-scripted theatre excepted. See Chapter 17.

ceremonies, I saw that most people don't take the competition aspect seriously, but mainly see it as an excuse to celebrate. Since then I've entered some competitions, and adjudicated others, and enjoyed their festive nature and the opportunity they give artists to present their work. Just don't take it too seriously if you lose—or if you win.

15

Rehearsal and Performance

Start to let go

So, now, let's assume you've succeeded in getting a production, and you're going into rehearsal. Any parent will understand this next bit. The task of the playwright in rehearsal resembles the task of every parent watching their kids growing up. It's the painful art of letting go.

A few years ago, I was at a party, shortly before beginning rehearsals for a new play I'd written. The other guests included Kathryn MacKay, the play's director, and her husband Greg Wanless, a fellow theatre artist. I was telling another guest, "Kathryn's directing my new play!" Greg overheard me, and said, "Actually, John's written the script for *Kathryn's* new play."

He made an excellent point. In rehearsals, you'll discover that it no longer belongs to you. Begin to let go. You're not the boss in rehearsal. You're not even the boss in a workshop, although it exists for your benefit. The stage manager is the boss of organizing the time and space, and the director is the boss of how the actors do their work. This relationship, too, is enshrined in the Playwrights Guild (PGC) / PACT contract, in a clause that says, "The Playwright shall at all times pay due consideration to the Producer's and/or the Director's authority at the place of rehearsal." The one area where you *are* the boss is the choice of words spoken by the actors, and we'll get back to that shortly.

You may find that as rehearsals continue, the actors form a unit which, deliberately or not, can seem to exclude others. The actors sometimes feel like soldiers on the front line, with the rest of us sending orders forward from our safe, comfortable positions in the rear. So you may have the disconcerting feeling, upon walking into the rehearsal room, that, although they welcome you politely, they don't need you anymore. You can feel somewhat shunned. In *Text and Context*, Greenblatt refers to "the natural camaraderie that will usually develop amongst a cast which, by definition, must exclude the director"[82]—and, even more, the playwright.

However, as another clause in those contracts says, "The Playwright shall have the right to attend rehearsals." Combine this right with the clause forbidding changes made without your consent, and the effect is that you're entitled to be involved and make the text changes you want. Let's hope you'll never need that legal protection; but its very existence encourages the assumption that the playwright is on the team. One does hear of directors (of productions outside the PGC / PACT agreement) who receive the playwright's script and say, "Okay, bye, see you on opening night." This is unacceptable, and those clauses are in the contract to prevent it.

However, there is the occasional playwright, like Australia's great TYA master Finegan Kruckemeyer, who chooses not to attend rehearsals, but just to show up on opening night and see what they've done with it. He writes:

> During the creation of a new commission [...] I always sit down for a development week or two with the ensemble [...] of collective unpacking of a draft [...] I believe all the necessary clues and demands should be embedded in the text and if something's missing, that's on me. [...] So I enjoy the surprise—of my colleagues' talents, of things in the play I didn't know were in the play, and of the great pleasure (the one which got me into this whole

---

82 *Text and Context*, 88.

profession) which is sitting in a story and watching a story told.[83]

Kruckemeyer adds that he often does attend rehearsals and/or do rewrites, on the company's request. In any case, most playwrights attend most or all of their rehearsals, and it's advisable for beginning playwrights to do the same, if possible, and take this opportunity to learn about the process.

Why not direct your own play?

First, yet again there are exceptions: some playwrights are good directors of their own work, and you may have to do so if there's nobody else available. But there's a misconception that you *should* direct your own play, because you understand it best. I disagree. Directing your own work, you can exaggerate the play's weaknesses. You want a director who will sympathize with what you're trying to do, but who may see the play with fresh eyes, and bring it unexpected ideas and fresh angles.

When my friend Jane Heyman directed one of my first plays, I was delighted by how in sync we were. In rehearsal, I'd think, "At this point that actor should walk over there and get angrier," and Jane would tell the actor, "Why don't you cross left, and let him get under your skin more." Why, it was as if I were directing the play myself! Later, I boasted about this to another director, and he said, "Oh, so *that's* what was wrong with that production."

Still later, I told this story to my mother, who tended to think in visual metaphors. Without having seen the play, she replied, "Well, of course the production seemed flat, if you and Jane agreed too much. After all, *you need two eyes to perceive depth.*" (Emphasis mine, because that's so good that I want you to really notice it.)

I brought my mother's observation back to Jane, who loved it. We agreed that whenever we worked together we would be sure to disagree about at least one thing. Since then, in the other productions we've done together, whenever we've caught ourselves disagreeing,

---

83   Private e-mail to the author, Sept. 20, 2022.

we have had a brief celebration of the fact—"Yay, we found our disagreement!"—sometimes to the puzzlement of the actors.[84]

Rewriting in rehearsal

The chief reason to attend rehearsals—especially for a premiere production—is to do script rewrites. As you know by now, a main purpose of this book is to teach you how to minimize those last-minute rewrites; but it's a safe bet that you'll have some anyway. The first few days of rehearsal don't just *look* like script workshops: often they sort of *are*. Some directors schedule in extra time for the playwright's rewrites. And it is unwise to go into production if the script is not at least more or less finished.

Come into rehearsal with your own paper copy of the script on which to scribble. Yes, paper—for the actors, director, and stage manager, too. It's distressing to see actors wasting rehearsal time scrolling frantically to find their place in scripts on their tablets, or, worse, their phones. This is not a Luddite attitude: computers are miraculous inventions, appropriate for many tasks, including writing the play at home. But the appropriate technology for rehearsal, whatever your job, is with your nice big 8½-by-11-inch script on paper, and pencil in hand. Both you and the actors need that palimpsest—a personal scribbled record, in pencil, of the changes you've made—and a physical sense of which page you're on.

You may want to go to the director on the first day of rehearsal, especially in premiere productions, and ask for a deadline: the last day when you'll be allowed to bring in rewrites. This is to protect the cast from you: to give them a moment when they'll finally know that *this* is the script they'll be performing on opening night, and they won't have any more changes to memorize. In practice, it seems to work well to place that deadline at the end of the week before tech week.

Besides the rewrites that you yourself notice are needed, a rewrite may be requested by an actor, if a different wording is more

---

84 Jane insists that I quoted my mother to her as saying "you need binocular vision to perceive depth." However, I insist that my mother said "two eyes." So we've agreed that we have found our disagreement for this book.

comfortable for them. Certainly, you can agree, but if you still think it works better your way, you have the right to (politely) stick to your guns. And you may have the gratifying experience of changing a line for an actor, and then seeing them discover that it worked better the first time.

It's usually assumed that you'll go home at the end of the day, finish any remaining rewrites in the evening, and bring them in the next morning. There's nothing wrong with saying, "Yeah, okay, this needs a rewrite, you'll have it tomorrow." On such occasions the director should allow you time the next morning to either dictate or hand out the new rewrites. You dictate the shorter rewrites—a change of a word or two or a line or two—for the actors, director and stage manager to scribble into their scripts. For extensive rewrites that take over much of a page or more, it's best to reprint the pages, with copies for everybody.

When you dictate the small changes to the cast, be precise: announce exactly which words to cut and which new words to insert, and then read them the resultant new line. Give them time to write the new stuff in. I recommend that you include line numbers in your rehearsal scripts: they are very useful for locating these smaller changes that you dictate.

Don't be embarrassed by the apparent pettiness of some changes: "Replace 'I'm gonna go' with 'I'm going.'" Actors know that such changes are often about rhythm, tone, and what sounds right to the playwright. Occasionally you may be asked why you're making a specific change. It's perfectly valid to reply, "Because it sounds better."

For those larger changes, where you're reprinting a whole page or series of them, make that a separate file and write one of those running heads or "Headers and Footers," mentioned in Chapter 12, with the play's title, your name, the date, and the page numbers: "*Totally Nana's Ride*, John Lazarus, June 28/2015 rewrite, p. 6-7." After the production closes, you can then collate those rewritten pages into the script to make a presentable new draft to send out in search of further productions.

Giving notes

Give your notes to the director, not the actors. Giving notes directly to the actors is an insult to your director and violates the sacred principle that everybody in the production should stick to their own job. It also places an extra burden on the actors, who have enough to deal with from one director: they don't need two.

The one kind of note you *may* give straight to an actor is when the actor is actually saying the wrong words, and the stage manager hasn't noticed or is too busy with other tasks. Even then, I wait until the actor's made the same mistake three times, so that it's in danger of becoming a habit. Almost always, the actor will apologize and thereafter get it right, or, as noted above, may ask you to change the line to their version, in which case it's your call.

Regarding all your other concerns that come up in rehearsal, your task is to write them down, and then go off with the director (and stage manager, if available), for a coffee, a meal, or a beer—and offer two kinds of notes.

One kind is proposed rewrites. "I'm going to change this line so that it's less obvious / more obvious / angrier / less angry / a bit longer so the actor can get to the door / a bit shorter because the actor's already at the door," etc. That's the playwright's prerogative, though, of course, if the director disagrees, he's free to say so, and useful discussion can follow.

The other notes are "humble directorial suggestions" on matters of interpretation. They really should be humble: offered not to protect your masterpiece, but as a recommendation from somebody who knows the script intimately. If a moment has been directed differently from the way you intended it, and you really think your initial idea would work better, you can say something like, "What I originally meant here was…" A good director who disagrees will try both interpretations at the next rehearsal, and it usually becomes instantly clear which one is preferable.

Expect your director to accept most but not all of your notes. A director agreeing with all your notes will not necessarily result in the best production. (See Jane Heyman, above.) They probably shouldn't reject all your notes either—although the one time a director rejected every note I gave him, the result was one of the best productions of a play of mine I've ever seen. Make of that what you will.

More about working with directors

There's a stereotype, enshrined in some old movies about theatre, that in professional rehearsals with truly talented people, everybody's at each other's throats. The director greets the cast on Day One with something like, "You'll bleed, you'll cry, you'll hate me, but in the end, by God, we'll have a show!" Cut to a week later, with the director and playwright bellowing at each other and throwing pages in the air while the actors stand around looking weary.

If theatre people do this at all, it's because they're insecure. If the director is any good, what little arguing there is is friendly. Some of the finest directors are so easy-going and non-temperamental that you don't notice how brilliant they are until you see the results. It's part of a director's job to set the tone of the rehearsal, and good directors set a tone that is focused, energetic, cooperative, positive, and serious, though not without frequent laughter.

With any disagreement, what matters is not who wins but what works. It can be liberating to "win" an argument by turning on a dime and saying, "You're right, I was wrong, let's do it your way." This behaviour can give you a good reputation as one who works and plays well with others. Try not only to be that kind of theatre artist, but also to work with other artists who behave that way too.

Stick to your own job

> The first step in solving a problem is to figure out whether it's your problem or not.
> —My late father, Rupert Lazarus

The advice against playwrights giving notes to actors is one example of the larger principle that everybody in the theatre stick to their own jobs. For other examples, it is bad form for actors to give each other directorial notes, and good directors avoid "giving a line reading," which means saying, "Say the line like this," and dictating the tone of voice—in other words, doing the actors' acting for them.

This is good advice even, or especially, when you have some expertise in the job that somebody else is doing on this production. Most people who survive in this business are "slashes": playwright / director / actor, etc. So you may be acting in a play that you think you could direct better than the director, or directing on a set you would have designed differently. It doesn't matter. Don't tell other people how to do their job, even if you actually *know* how to do their job. Today you're just the playwright.

However, my father's dictum, above, doesn't necessarily mean that if it's not your problem, you automatically stay out of it. You then have the option of deciding whether to step in or not. In the rehearsal room, the answer is usually "No," except on such rare occasions as when the director says, "Okay, I'm stumped. Ideas, anybody?"

In any case, the general rule against meddling in other people's tasks leads us to another form of doing so, which has become a bit of a fad. It's an actor's sin, not a playwright's, but it's a sin against playwrights, so don't let actors do it. It's called **paraphrasing**.

> Let those that play your clowns speak no more than is set down for them [...] That's villainous, and shows a most pitiful ambition in the fool that uses it.
> —Shakespeare, *Hamlet*, Act 3, Sc. 1

> As God is my witness, I'll never paraphrase again!
> —Producer / director / writer / actor Marvin Kaye, as an Acting student at Studio 58, in rehearsals for his first play as a playwright

Paraphrasing is that thing some actors do in rehearsal, when they glance at their next line of dialogue in the script, look their acting partner in the eye, and improvise a line similar to what the playwright put on the page, only different—on the unspoken grounds that the actual choice of words doesn't matter. Well, the actual choice of words matters.

The play is the words in the script. If they're not rehearsing the words in the script, they're not rehearsing your play, but are wasting precious rehearsal time showing off how cleverly they can improvise dialogue. If you're not hearing your actual words spoken, you won't know how to improve them. Also, the actor may change the entire meaning of a passage without realizing it. Finally, it's an insult to the playwright, implying that even under the pressure of doing an entirely different job, the actor has enough brain power left over to casually improvise lines that are better than what the playwright created over a period of months.

Improvising dialogue is appropriate in some contexts: in devised theatre, and sometimes briefly, as an exercise to figure out why a scene isn't working. Some actors will paraphrase for just a few days of rehearsal, and then settle down and learn their lines, and if that's okay with you, well, it's your play. I would still argue that they aren't rehearsing the play until they start rehearsing the play. One more time: the power to insist on which words are spoken is the only actual power the playwright has in rehearsal. Use it wisely, but use it.

Tech week and previews

Tech week is the final week before an audience comes in, when the elements of lighting, sound, costumes, makeup, hair, props, and sets are introduced or touched up. **Previews** are the final rehearsals, which take place in front of an audience.

By tech week your deadline should be past, and your work essentially finished. But stick around and watch the fascinating process, especially if you're new to the business. Also, deadlines notwithstanding, there may be moments when your skills are still required to fix a problem that was not apparent until tech time. I once cut an entire scene and two characters during previews, when it became clear that the scene was both unnecessary and out of character for the heroine. (Fortunately, the two actors were playing several characters each, so instead of being fired, they simply had fewer costume changes.) On another occasion I added a new speech at the director's request, to give actors time for a backstage costume change whose difficulty had not been foreseen until they were in costume.

You've had years to write your play; the director, designers, composer, and choreographer have had months to work on it; the actors have had weeks to rehearse. Now, during tech week, the crew has a couple of days in which to do their jobs. Keep out of their way. Don't be a diva. It's not your baby any more. If you really think some aspect of the tech is getting in the way of something you've been trying to do, you might take it up quietly with the director or stage manager. But think carefully before you raise an objection. There will always be something that someone else has contributed to the production that will not be to your taste. But it's a collaborative art form. Get over yourself. I guarantee you, something in your script will not be entirely to the taste of somebody else in the show. Try to enjoy, or at least be curious about, the surprises that come up in tech week.

Be in the audience during **previews**: those first few performances, at reduced ticket prices, before the official opening night. Previews are everybody's chance to find out how things go with the introduction of the most important "character," the audience. The feeling is similar to the first time you heard your dialogue out loud, and the first time you heard them in front of an audience at a reading. Once again, everything sounds different.

Sit in the audience, near the back or off to the side, and take notes. After the performance, when the director gathers cast and crew for his own notes, sit with them, and listen and scribble. He'll give them some of the same notes you wrote down, and some others you never thought of. Then politely approach him afterwards with any notes that you think are important but that he missed.

Previews mark a milestone for your play, in that they usually include the first paying audience. The moment when people first fork over some actual money to watch a play, it ceases to be defined as a work in progress and—whether or not there are still changes to be made—becomes, for better or worse, the work of art.

Selling the production

Theatres have publicity departments, whose job it is to decide what it is about your play that will appeal to an audience, and to sell it on that basis. Suddenly other writers, often strangers to you, are summing up your play in terms of what will get the public's attention. After months or years of looking at your play from every possible angle, you may find it being described in terms which never occurred to you, and which seem to have little or no relation to what you've been trying to do.

Again, as with so many aspects of the job once the script is more or less finished, your job is, generally speaking, to keep out of it. If the P.R. people are describing your play in terms that don't seem accurate to you, you may console yourself with the thought that once they've done their job of getting the bums into the seats, then the eyes and ears attached to those bums will get the play you intended. Or, indeed, you may discover that the publicists' take on your play is a new, legitimate one, just as you may have discovered fresh takes on your script from the actors' interpretations. Of course, if they seriously misread your play and write a real distortion of it, you'll want to speak up, but this is rare. It's their job to make your work look as good as possible.

Regarding billing, the PGC / PACT contract stipulates that the playwright's name will be mentioned in all publicity under the theatre's control regarding this particular play, including posters, programs and websites, and that nobody's name shall be printed in larger type than the playwright's. Theatre companies have sometimes been lax in this matter, but it's a sound principle.

Yet another clause from those contracts: "The Theatre may request the Playwright to make personal appearances and give personal interviews for purposes of publicity." Happily, the media do take an interest when a new play opens. So this will probably happen to you, whether your play is being produced by a professional company in a big city, a community theatre in a small town, or a group of students. You may be interviewed for radio, TV, a podcast or a newspaper, before opening. Or, during the run, they may ask you to take the stage after a performance to answer questions from the audience or be interviewed by a theatre staffer.

These demands usually come up at the most stressful time—just when you're finishing rewrites, and as the show is going into tech week—but publicity is a precious commodity, so seize those opportunities.

Be polite and friendly. Thank them for having you on. If it's TV or video, sit still and comfortably, without fidgeting. Smile, even on radio: it's audible in your voice. Answer the questions directly, but have an anecdote or two ready. If you're doing multiple interviews, don't tell the same story each time. Be prepared for some standard questions: what interested you in playwriting, what related work you've done, what inspired you to write this one. Don't ramble on: better too brief than too lengthy. Give your co-workers much credit and be modest but confident about your contribution. Never speak rudely about anybody else involved with the production: sooner or later, such rudeness will come back and get you.

Opening night...

On the day of opening night, buy cards and/or small, in-jokey gifts that relate to the play, for cast, crew, and office staff. This will help distract you from your inevitable jitters. Then, at the **half** (the time when the actors are required to be in the building, 35 minutes before curtain), you can run around to the dressing rooms, distributing your cards and telling everybody to break a leg.

Enjoy the opening night performance. Listen to the audience. Don't make notes. It's too late. There's nothing you can do now but have a good time.

Enjoy the party afterwards. Congratulate everybody. Keep telling them how great they were tonight. Comfort that actor who dried for three seconds and thank the actor whose ad-lib saved the day. When talking to friends who were in the audience, keep asking, "And how are *you* these days?" It's not about you any more, if indeed it ever was.

When people congratulate you, thank them, and don't tell them what went wrong. Very often, those involved in the production see a performance quite differently from those in the audience. If audience members liked it better than you did, don't argue with them.

On the other hand, don't take criticisms too seriously either. At two different opening-night parties, two different friends have cheerfully told me that they hated my play! I don't know what to tell you to do if that happens. Me, I laughed.

...And the morning after, including reviews

> It's taken me decades, but I never read reviews anymore when I am working as an actor; not even after the show has closed.
>
> —Richard Greenblatt[85]

Reviews by critics in daily newspapers are becoming a thing of the past, along with the newspapers themselves, but in some cities you can still get up the next morning, buy a paper and find out what the local reviewer thought of your play. However, the business of theatre criticism has changed greatly in the last few years.

There is now both more and less criticism than there used to be, and the old saying "Everyone's a critic" is truer than ever. There are fewer professionals, and more ordinary folks weighing in on blogs, Facebook, etc. In this atmosphere, the comments you receive will probably skew towards the favourable. You're likely to have more friends wanting to promote your play and say good things about it than detractors dumping on it. On the other hand, the detractors, especially the anonymous ones, can be harsh. Pay no attention to anonymous trolls. If they don't have the courage to put their names on their opinions, they are unworthy of your notice.

The movie cliché of learning, the morning after opening night, that the play is a "hit" or a "flop" is now pretty much an urban legend. Those terms reflect an old-fashioned way of thinking about theatre, and anyway, most plays fall somewhere in between. Often, you can't tell right away what effect your play has had or will have. On the morning after the premiere opening of what became my most successful play, I was at a loss to figure out from the mixed reviews what we had here. It wasn't until months later, when the play began getting more productions, that I began to think it would do well.

Many artists think professional criticism should not exist: Greenblatt calls it a "bane on our art form."[86] This is understandable. It is infuriating when a person with few or no qualifications—and the sad fact is that most critics are under-qualified—takes one

---

85 *Text and Context*, 143.

86 *Text and Context*, 144.

look at the fruits of your years of labour, and then, usually under deadline pressure, dashes off a public opinion which can affect your livelihood.

On the other hand (and speaking as a former critic myself), it is a legitimate art form, and, when practised conscientiously, can be helpful to everyone: as a consumer report to the potential audience, an indication to the artists of how their work is received, and a placing of the work in various contexts: the era, the artists' other work, and the art form in general.

However, it's probably not good for your emotional health or for the development of your art to take criticism too seriously. You may choose, like Greenblatt, not to read reviews, but I suggest you keep them all: good, bad, and indifferent. It's easy to overestimate their importance, early in your career, but they may give you a few laughs later in life. This is one advantage to getting older: the first review you get constitutes 100% of your reviews, but the hundredth review constitutes 1%. Sir John Gielgud said that over the years, the paper they're printed on develops a comfortingly brittle, yellow quality.

Never write angry letters to the editor or the website in response to a bad review of your work. It will alert people who missed the original review to the fact that you got a bad review, and maybe send them back to read it. And it will make some people think that if the review hurt your feelings that much, then there must have been some truth to it.

You've opened—now what?

Go back and see the play a few times in front of different audiences. It's a great learning experience. Notice how it evolves between its opening and closing performances, as the actors find meanings in your text that they (and maybe you) hadn't noticed before, and as they learn how audiences respond to specific moments.

After the run closes, sit down with the paper script containing those small changes you scribbled and the larger ones you retyped, and type and collate the computer files into a coherent new draft of the play. Now you can include a "Production History" in the introductory pages, citing the theatre company, location and dates, and listing the original cast, crew, and creative team. (See Chapter 6, *Totally Nana's Ride*, for an example.)

Then it's time to send it to other theatres. You still shouldn't boast in the cover letter about what a masterpiece it is, but now that it's been produced, some quotations from your more positive reviews—or a quote from the artistic director or general manager—may help to sell it.

You may also try to get the play published. Admittedly, to most playwrights, the higher priority is to get more productions. Plays published in book form don't normally sell in large quantities, and, frankly, seeing your work in front of an audience is more exciting than simply knowing that people are sitting at home reading it.

But on the other hand, it is gratifying to see your play preserved in a nicely designed book with your name on it; the fact looks good in your resumé; it makes your play eligible for some awards; and your friends and family will be impressed, especially the ones who have never seen your plays and aren't sure exactly what it is that you do.

A few publishing houses in Canada specialize in stage plays, including Playwrights Canada Press, Talonbooks, and the fine publisher of this book you're reading right now, J. Gordon Shillingford Publishing, which publishes plays under its Scirocco Drama imprint. And the Playwrights Guild of Canada also puts out inexpensive publications of plays written by its members. Buy some! Read them!

The protocol for sending plays to the publishers is similar to that of sending them to the theatres, with at least one important difference. This small number of publishers are less specialized than the theatres, and have a wider range in terms of what they will consider. A single publisher will consider all sorts of plays, from TYA to sophisticated adult material.

The Biz (Such As It Is)

I have always felt it was too bad that you could make a killing, but not a living, in the theater.

—Robert Anderson

ELAINE STRITCH: And what do you do, Darling?
ME: I'm a playwright.
STRITCH: Oh, *that's* an easy way to make a living!

—Conversation in a downtown Vancouver shopping mall, late 1990s

Very few Canadians make a living as playwrights; the rest of us supplement our incomes with other work, including, if we're lucky, teaching. However, plays do earn money for their authors, if not usually in large amounts, so the business side of this art form is a worthy topic.

Copyright

This information on copyright makes no claim to be complete. There are many books and websites that will tell you more. Copyright law is different in different places, and this is not legal advice and should not be construed as such.

Under Canadian common law, everything you write, including an e-mail to your cousin, is immediately copyright in your name, as soon as you write it, whether you put the word "Copyright" on it or not. We touched on this in Chapter 2, in the context of your adapting *other* people's work. Now we're talking about *your* copyright.

On the title page of your play, you want to write "Copyright © Joe Blow, 2023," or whatever. In Word, the © is created by typing (c) or inserting it as a symbol. You might also want to add, "All Rights Reserved," which means "You can't do *anything* with this without checking with me first"—just to scare them a little.

Really, that's all you need to do. There are more elaborate ways to protect your copyright—such as mailing a sealed copy of the manuscript to one's lawyer or notary as proof of prior possession—but most writers I know don't bother with these. The explosive proliferation of fiction in our time has made it harder and harder to prove ownership of an idea: a character trait, a plot point, an interesting setting, an unprecedented theme. These days, dialogue must be nearly identical to someone else's before anyone dares use the word "plagiarism."

In any case, outright plagiarism is a rare event. The more common infraction is for a company (usually of students or amateurs) to produce your play, with your name on it, but to fail to get around to asking you or sending you royalties. However, this too seems less frequent these days, when it's easier to track down playwrights and agents on the Internet. What has not changed is a widespread belief that if a group doesn't charge admission, they don't need to pay you anything. If it's a public performance, they still need your permission, and you can still insist on a royalty payment. You can decide to let them do it for free, but that's your choice, not theirs. (If you have an agent, they too must be involved in such decisions. More on agents below.)

The use of your work in the classroom is another matter. Drama could hardly be taught in schools if teachers couldn't use scenes from established plays. So to make plays affordable to schools, Canada has an agency called Access Copyright, which pays annual fees to authors and artists to compensate them for the use of their work in the classroom. The fees are calculated based on the number of works each author has published. It's a rough approximation, but it beats the heck out of getting paid nothing. Writers must register with the agency to be eligible. Other countries have similar programs.

A final note on this: do not sell or, worse, give away, the copyright to your play. Film and TV operate differently: the production company usually owns the script. But in theatre, you probably won't ever be asked to trade away your copyright, but if you ever are, don't. I suppose you *might* want to consider it if they offered enough money to retire on *and* to console you for what they'd do to your script, but even then, think long and hard about it.

The Playwrights Guild

As mentioned several times earlier, there's a national organization that you should know about, called the Playwrights Guild of Canada,[87] devoted to the protection and promotion of Canadian playwrights and plays, and to advocacy on our behalf. You can find their website at https://playwrightsguild.ca. As this is being written, the PGC has more than 800 members.

The Guild promotes our plays by making them available on its website (www.canadianplayoutlet.com): currently over 3,000 titles, with authors' profile pictures and bios. It produces the abovementioned Tom Hendry Awards,[88] including an "Emerging Playwright Award" for early career artists. Members can also take part in the PlayConnect Program, which pays us to give public readings of our works. And the Guild puts out a monthly newsletter, free to members, announcing that month's readings and productions of members' plays.

---

87 *Sic*: no apostrophe. I don't know why. They're a very literate bunch, otherwise. It used to be called the Playwrights Union of Canada, so if you come across old material with that name on it, that's the same organization.

88 Tom Hendry (1929–2012) was a playwright and theatre administrator who co-founded four of the most important theatre institutions in this country—the Playwrights Guild, the Manitoba Theatre Centre, Toronto Free Theatre, and the Banff Playwrights' Colony—and also served as the first literary manager of the Stratford Festival. He was a kind, witty, charming, and altogether lovely gentleman.

The Guild has negotiated, and triennially revisits and updates, the set of standard contracts with the Professional Association of Canadian Theatres that I've been quoting. This is so that we don't have to reinvent the wheel every time a playwright walks into the office of a theatre that's going to do their new play. The Guild can advise you on contracts and on your rights as an artist, and can go to bat for you if you get into a dispute with a theatre. Again, as noted earlier, the mere existence of these contracts means that such disputes are rare, but it's great to know that this large organization has your back.

Its website provides access to professional development opportunities, including jobs, workshops, and webinars. As a member you'll be invited to all Guild events, including the annual conference and annual general meeting, and you can stand for office on their National Forum and various committees. As this is being written, full membership for playwrights costs $155 per year, supporting membership costs $35, and student membership is $20 (all in Canadian dollars, plus HST).

Agents

An agent has two tasks: to help get the play produced, by sending it to theatre companies and talking it up; and, when it does get produced, to negotiate the contract. Some playwrights have agents and some do not. If you're willing to do your own mailings, feel confident about negotiating your own contracts, and don't mind putting in the work, you can save yourself the agent's percentage. However, for those of us too busy, lazy, or unsure of our skills in these areas, it's a pleasure to give this part of the work to someone who enjoys it and is good at it. A shrewd agent with dramaturgical skills can also be a great source of advice and encouragement. And another advantage to having an agent is that although, as mentioned earlier, it's considered poor taste to write a cover letter saying, "I personally believe that this is one of the best new Canadian plays to come along in years," your agent can say so for you.

There are not a great many playwrights' agents in Canada, and there seems to be no set way to find one. You can ask around at your regional script development centre or within your informal community of fellow playwrights. The Playwrights Guild of Canada can serve as an agent for amateur productions. And one of the ways that you'll know your latest play is a success is if one or more agents contact *you*.

Agents usually collect a fee of 10% or 15% of the money you make from a production. (So, if your royalty is 10% of the box office, and the agent's fee is 10% or 15% of your royalty, she's making 1% to 1.5% of the box office. It may not sound like much, but a good agent with several clients can do well, and most playwrights' agents also represent screenwriters.) Many of them collect this fee for everything of yours that gets produced, whether they negotiate the contract or not. Others may insist on negotiating all your contracts, even if your production is a simple matter between friends. And then there are some agents who stay out of it if your friend wants to do a one-act of yours and pay you a straight 10% of the box office, and some agents who collect their percentage only on the stuff they negotiate for you.

So how much are we talking about here?

Let's assume you've landed a production and are going to talk with the good people at the theatre company that wants to produce your play. What's the deal?

In Canada, the standard royalty fee paid to a playwright for a **premiere production**—the first production of a play—is 10% of the box office take. With a medium-sized theatre, you'll probably make a few thousand dollars from a typical production Technically, that 10% is the minimum, though theatres seldom pay more. (They do pay 12% for musicals, because the royalties are usually split among a playwright, composer, and lyricist.) In theory there are no minimums for **stock contracts**—contracts for productions following the first one—but in practice, 98% of theatres belonging to the Professional Association of Canadian Theatres will pay 10% as a matter of course. There are formulas for figuring out what fraction of a season ticket price will constitute part of that box office revenue, and that amount should be factored in.

In the U.S., the theatres tend to pay between 6% and 8% of the box office. One particular playwright / composer / lyricist of a current record-breaking Broadway hit is rumoured to be collecting 3% of the box office as his royalty. He's still making millions, but in principle, this seems unbalanced.

Usually, the theatre pays the playwright a minimum amount in advance. Traditionally this amount represents 10% of what the theatre would receive if your play were performed in front of an audience filling 60% of the theatre's capacity. Then, when the play is produced, and the theatre calculates how much actually came in, they deduct this advance from your royalties. But if your play earns less than 60% of the theatre's total potential—even if the production is cancelled—you are still legally entitled to that 10% of 60%.

A **commission** is a deal whereby a theatre pays you extra in advance, *not* deductible from your later royalties but just to help you get by while you're writing the play, and, in return, get to produce it first (or reject it: the commission does not obligate them to produce). Currently, the minimum set rate for commissions is $3,060 CDN.

The Playwrights Guild and PACT have worked out other kinds of contracts as well, to cover such different situations as amateur productions, TYA theatres that tour their plays to schools, etc.

Theatre people to be wary of

When you deal with a theatre, you'll be talking with the company's **general manager**, or **G.M.**, who takes care of the business end: applying for the grants and corporate donations, making the budgets, estimating and then calculating the box office revenue, signing the contracts, etc. The **artistic director**, or **A.D.**, chooses the plays for the season, oversees rehearsals and performances, and usually directs some of the productions herself. Sometimes these two are the same person, often called the **artistic producer**. In any case, you'll be dealing with the general manager, whatever her official title.

With very few, rare exceptions, general managers of Canadian theatres deal honestly, care about the quality of the work, and want you and everyone else to be happy working with them. But occasionally, sleazy types do crop up in live theatre. And there may also be some who are not actually trying to con you, but are new to the profession and make mistakes out of ignorance.

Beware of G.M.s who tell you that their theatre company is doing you a favour, and/or taking a chance on you, by producing your play for free, or for less than the standard 10% of the box office. You could argue that *you're* doing *them* a favour, and/or taking a chance on them, by letting them take 90% of "your" box office money, and you're not going to let them take more.

Sometimes they may ask you to donate your play for free on the grounds that they're offering you "exposure." Singer/songwriter Connie Kaldor, who hails from Regina, has a great answer for that: "Where I come from, people *die* of exposure."

Here's the basic principle: through law and common usage, your play has a royalty attached to it. In return for the effort you made to (a) learn how to write these things in the first place and then (b) write one that they want, you are entitled to a specific amount of money whenever the play is performed for an audience, even for free admission. So a theatre that asks you to donate your play for free is asking that you, as a punishment for writing the play, be the person selected to donate your own royalty money.

Of course, as mentioned above, you can, sometimes, choose or offer to waive your royalties. This is a kind of donation to their theatre, so you can do it as such: agree in advance that you'll donate the royalty fee back to them. You get listed as one of their donors, get a receipt, get any other perks they give to donors, and deduct it from your taxes as a charitable donation.

In any case, your work has value. If it has enough value for someone to want to produce it, then it has enough value to be paid for—certainly at the modest rates paid to playwrights.

Finally on this topic, here's one more piece of business advice, courtesy of my late father, Rupert Lazarus, which applies in any field, and has saved my skin more than once: If they won't give you 24 hours to decide whether to sign—don't sign.

A final note on the biz: It ain't easy

Don't be too disappointed if, after all this work, your play gets one production and then fades from public view. These days, achieving even a second production is considered notable success for a Canadian play. Since the artistic director's job of designing a season includes a great many factors besides the quality of the scripts, don't take it personally if your play is not selected.

If you're truly dedicated to this art form, you'll probably be hammering away at the next play, even while you're sending the previous one to other theatres. Do that a couple of times, and get a couple of productions of your plays, and one day someone will pleasantly surprise you by referring to your "career."

17

Other Forms

Devised Theatre, Theatre of the Real, and Theatre with Differently Abled Artists

Most of this book has followed the traditional approach to theatre creation, whereby the playwright sits at home and writes a script for two or more characters and then brings it into rehearsal and makes further changes. A number of forms currently offer alternatives to that approach. This chapter takes a quick look at some of those.

Some kinds of plays may be directed and staged differently from the conventional stuff, and may *appear* quite different, but are written in the traditional way—such as the solo show, theatre for young audiences, site-specific theatre, live/digital blends, immersive theatre, and even the musical. But in this chapter we'll look at forms that really do require a different kind of work from the playwright: devised theatre, theatre of the real, and theatre involving differently abled artists. This book can offer no more than a brief glance at these forms, which are described in detail in other books, papers, and websites.

Devised theatre

Devised theatre is created by the cast in rehearsal, rather than written by a solitary playwright in advance. This seems an awkward name for it, as all theatre is, of course, devised. Paul Thompson of Toronto's Theatre Passe Muraille, which has specialized in such work, calls it "collective creation."

The task of the designated "playwright," if there is one, can take any form between doing most of the traditional playwriting, and serving as little more than a rehearsal typist. Between those two extremes lie varying amounts of the work of dramaturging and shaping the material invented by the actors. Sometimes, developing a devised play replicates the central thesis of this book—the two ways about it—in that the playwright or team of playwrights constructs the plot, while the cast members improvise the dialogue. And often, part of your job and theirs will be to *define* your job and theirs, sometimes in midstream, as your task may change as the piece evolves. They might ask you to take a more active part in shaping the story. Or to butt out more.

Theatre of the real

Sometimes called "verbatim theatre" and sometimes "docudrama," **theatre of the real** portrays real historical or current events, and uses, for some or all of its text, real conversations by real people. Due to its less-scripted nature, it overlaps considerably with devised theatre. Again, the function of the "playwright" is open to wide interpretation: from conventional playwriting, to being a dramaturge of transcribed material for the actors to work with, to being the typist who transcribes the recorded conversations.

Well-known examples include *The Farm Show* (1976), by Theatre Passe Muraille, about the life of farmers in Southwestern Ontario; *The Laramie Project* (2000), by New York's Tectonic Theater Project and playwright Moisés Kaufman, about the murder of gay teenager Matthew Shepard; *London Road* (2011), a British opera about a neighbourhood in Ipswich responding to the news of a serial killer; and *Out the Window* (2018), a Canadian work by Liza

Balkan, based on her witnessing a police beating. All these derive their scripts from news accounts, court transcripts, and interviews with ordinary people.

The Farm Show deserves special mention as both theatre of the real and devised theatre, which used radical, cutting-edge staging techniques to tell the stories of a rather conservative community, resulting in an enormous hit with both the farmers who inspired it and the city folk who saw it across Canada. Passe Muraille member Ted Johns, credited with "prepar[ing]" the script, sums up the process elegantly by writing, "Usually the script is the first hint of a play's existence. In this case, it is the last."[89]

A more recent example, and of a different kind of theatre of the real, is *Winners and Losers* (2012), created and performed by Vancouver artists Marcus Youssef and James Long. In that play, partly scripted and partly improvised, they present themselves to the audience as "Marcus" and "Jamie," playing a game about labelling different persons, places or things as "winners" or "losers." When they get down to arguing about whether they themselves are winners or losers, the audience gets uncomfortable, not knowing how much of the show is "theatre" and how much is "real," and to what extent, if any, these two actors' real friendship is being threatened.

And that is part of the point of theatre of the real: to disorient the audience and move us out of that comfortable place in the darkened auditorium where we can securely assume that what we're seeing is fiction. Instead, we experience that "Insecurity" that provides the title of Jenn Stephenson's book on theatre of the real—and in which, not surprisingly, she devotes a good deal of eloquent commentary to *Winners and Losers*.

Working with differently abled artists

An illuminating trend has recently grown very popular: theatre showcasing individuals who have not traditionally had access to the stage, including work written, devised, and acted by artists

89 Theatre Passe Muraille / Paul Thompson, *The Farm Show* (Toronto: Coach House Press, 1976), 7.

with Down syndrome and other such cognitive differences from the majority of people.

In Vancouver, Marcus Youssef and Niall McNeil have co-written and acted in plays greeted with much acclaim.[90] Youssef is mentioned just above as one of the creators of *Winners and Losers*, and McNeil is a fellow playwright and actor who has Down syndrome. In Toronto, Judith Thompson has worked with differently abled performers in a company called Rare Theatre, to create several original shows. In Kingston, director Kathryn MacKay has worked with H'Art Studios and her own company, PeerLess Productions, to create and develop original works written or co-written by playwrights with Down syndrome and other developmental challenges. And Vancouver's Theatre Terrific, whose members have a wide range of different mental and physical abilities, has been going strong since the 1980s.

These plays tend to operate by slightly different rules from those of neurotypical playwrights, and sometimes reflect the world as seen through the perceptions of their creators. At the risk of stereotyping them, I will say that in my experience these plays tend to be surreal, subversive, satirical, rude, boisterous, intelligent, full of surprises, and usually very funny.

There is also, currently, an explosion of new dance and theatre by artists with physical disabilities. *Skydive* (2010) was commissioned by Vancouver actor Bob Frazer and written by Kevin Kerr to be performed by the able-bodied Frazer and his quadriplegic colleague James Sanders. Using so-called "aerial choreography" technology developed by Victoria's Sven Johansson, the play depicts their two characters falling through space.[91]

Not only do the creators of these theatre pieces deserve the respect of having them shown to the general public and assessed on their own merits, but the rest of us owe it to ourselves to experience them. And if you get a chance to write for such a company, consider it an opportunity to learn a lot from some very interesting people.

90 Niall McNeil and Marcus Youssef, *King Arthur's Night and Peter Panties: A Collaboration Across Perceptions of Cognitive Difference* (Vancouver: Talonbooks, 2018).

91 Kevin Kerr, *Skydive* (Vancouver: Talonbooks, 2010).

18

Inspirational Wrap-up and Happy Ending

Stuff we haven't had a chance to talk about

In the classroom, peripheral topics come up and we get to go on tangents and explore them together. These tangents often include some of the most valuable lessons for both the students and me. But in writing this book, I've tried to stick to the subjects at hand. So this last chapter will consist of an assortment of side topics I haven't got to elsewhere.

The care and feeding of your inner playwright

You may start to feel as though you have a small animal inside you that does the actual writing, or perhaps a little piece of machinery, chugging along. You have to learn how to feed and take care of it: when to push it harder and when to let it take a break—when to construct plot and when to improvise dialogue—when to listen to others' advice and when to strike out on your own—when to put your current play aside and work on that other one—when to deal with other issues in your life and when to close the door and write. The only way to learn these things is through experience. And, of course, the way to get experience is by doing it well, doing it badly, and eventually figuring out which is which.

I once met the daughter of one of the pioneer Canadian playwrights mentioned in the Introduction. Her chief childhood memory of her father was the closed study door, and her mother's admonitions not to make too much noise, because Daddy, the great writer, was working. At the time that I heard this story, my children were young, and I decided not to be that kind of father.[92] As a result, I've sometimes felt as though the writing has been in my spare time, squeezed between household chores, parenting, and teaching. Of course, very few of us have the luxury of being able to write all the time, without day jobs to work at and families to take care of. So it's a series of choices you have to make every day.

Writers have different needs, and our work habits vary. Some writers schedule their writing time; some, like me, don't. Some have rituals to focus their minds before they begin writing; some, like me, don't. Perhaps the rituals fit more comfortably into the routines of writers whose writing time is scheduled, because they know they're going to sit down now for an hour or two. If you're grabbing a couple of minutes between taking out the laundry and mowing the lawn, and you may be interrupted at any moment by the dog needing to go outside, it doesn't make much sense to take up some of those minutes with a Yoga sun salutation first. To others, however, such little ceremonies might be essential.

In any case, it's good to make your writing a habit, and to try to get some in every day. That "some" can be as little as one sentence, though of course one sentence can lead to many more. Joan MacLean, a high-school drama teacher in B.C., advised me to emphasize turning off your phone when you're writing. Henrik Ibsen: "When I am writing I must be alone; if I have eight characters of a drama to do with, I have society enough; they keep me busy; I must learn to know them."[93]

When you're not actively writing, your play will sit in the back of your head, quietly evolving. At the very least, it can be useful as something to think about when you've got nothing else to think about. As mentioned in Chapter 13, you may revisit it after an

---

92   Some members of my family may find this hilarious.

93   Quoted by Lajos Egri in *The Art of Dramatic Writing*, 33.

absence to find that it has solved some of its problems on its own—
or, admittedly, that they've got worse.

The art doesn't care

A sad fact is that the play doesn't care how hard you labour at it.
You can knock yourself out for weeks over a passage which will
take ten seconds onstage and won't work—indeed, which you may
finally decide to cut—or you can casually toss off a speech which a
total stranger will recite to you on the street decades later.[94] There
seems no predictable correlation between the amount of work you
put into a passage and its value at the end. Of course, the more
work you put in, the more practice you get and the better your
chances of success in the long term. It also helps greatly if you
love the process enough not to resent the labour—even if you've
worked on a script for literally years, only to have it rejected by
one and all.[95] When you can shrug at that outcome and say, "Well,
I learned a lot and enjoyed writing it," then (a) you're a true artist
and (b) you probably have a day job.

Writer's blocks, etc.

Try to reimagine your "writer's block" as a stepping-stone. Write
out the block. Often "writer's blocks" consist of two or more
options, all of which seem undesirable for different reasons. So
write that out: "If my character does this, then I can't have this part
of the plot. But if she does that instead, then I lose that other good
idea. Of course, if she does this and *then* that—" or "If she does
this *third* thing—" And so you may find yourself coming up with
a solution.

You can often have it both ways.

Sometimes, two different problems are each other's solutions in
disguise.

---

94 This has happened to me more than once.

95 This has happened to me more than once.

Sometimes you can give your problem to the character. Examples: While writing *The Late Blumer* (1984), I realized that maybe it wasn't that I hadn't figured out young Shelly's sexual orientation: maybe she hadn't. Our friend William may have puzzled over how long it was taking for Hamlet to get off his butt and kill Claudius, and so may have given Hamlet the problem, resulting in "O what a rogue and peasant slave am I!" (Act 2, Sc. 2) and "How all occasions do inform against me" (Act 4, Sc. 4), two of the greatest soliloquies in literature.

Success, Part 1:
How good you are is none of your business

Don't think about making art, just get it done. Let everyone else decide if it's good or bad, whether they love it or hate it. While they are deciding, make even more art.
> —Andy Warhol

What great ones do, the less will prattle of.
> —Shakespeare, *Twelfth Night*, Act 1, Sc. 2

What job is it of mine to go around wondering what other people's perceptions are? I have enough, dealing with my own.
> —Keith Richards, *My Life as a Rolling Stone*,
> Ep. 2 (Mercury Studios, 2022)

We never find out how good we are. There are plenty of unreliable guides. In school you are graded, and given or denied prizes; in the profession, you get good or bad reviews, awards or snubs, money or unemployment. It's easy to be affected by these indicators. Someone congratulates you on your latest work and you feel like a success; a website publishes a list of the important playwrights and you're not on it, and you feel invisible. Both feelings are illusory. Such indicators don't define your value in the world.

History is full of people hugely successful in their own lifetimes and subsequently gone from public consciousness. One example is Eugène Scribe, the most popular playwright of the 19th century, now all but forgotten. It is also full of apparent failures who became renowned and revered after their deaths. Vincent van Gogh comes to mind. So does John Kennedy Toole, whose novel *A Confederacy of Dunces* was universally rejected for publication, until after he had died by suicide at 31, whereupon his mother got it published, and it went on to win the Pulitzer Prize and become part of the canon of great American literature.

You may know people who are widely considered the best in their fields, but who consider themselves failures. Sometimes this takes the form of attractive modesty, and sometimes of self-destructive neurosis. You may also know people who have never accomplished much but who have a strong sense of their own merit. This too can take two forms: attractive self-confidence or obnoxious egotism. In any case, our opinions of ourselves seem to have no predictable correlation to what others think of us. The solution is, of course, to try to ignore both the responses of others and your own self-assessment. Best to concentrate on continuing—and finding joy in—the work.

Try not to get too discouraged by your failures. No offence, but I hope you'll have some failures: if you don't, it means you're not trying hard enough. Look at the work of artists you admire: it's almost guaranteed that you'll find they've had their fair share of flops. If you define yourself by your failures, you'll get discouraged. If you identify only with your successes, you'll risk turning into a narcissist. The fact that you will never know how good you are at your art form is probably a blessing, because *how good you are is none of your business.*

Success, Part 2:
Their success is your success

Your success depends on the quality of your work plus many other factors, primarily plain old dumb luck. You can control the quality of your work, but you can't control those other factors that will determine your access to fame, money, good reviews, and big audiences.

If you can't control your own success, you can control the success of other artists even less, so you might as well be a good sport and decide that their success is also your success. We may chuckle with rueful recognition at Gore Vidal's famously bitchy line, "It is not enough to succeed; others must fail"—we've probably all felt that way at one time or another—but in fact we're better off seeing our fellow playwrights not as rivals but as colleagues in our community.

My attitude about this was formed in the 1970s, when all Canadian playwrights struggled together for respect and recognition. When George Ryga's *The Ecstasy of Rita Joe* opened in Washington, D.C. in 1973, *New York Times* critic Julius Novick wrote in his review, "'Canadian playwright.' The words seem a little incongruous together, like 'Panamanian hockey player,' almost, or 'Lebanese fur-trapper.'"[96] In the face of such condescension we simply had to band together and support each other. Despite a change in that attitude among foreign critics, the intervening decades have provided no reason to revise that attitude. Cheering on your colleagues not only takes the sting out of seeing a fellow playwright enjoying a big hit when your latest masterpiece is going unproduced, but also helps keep you humble when you get a hit of your own.

Deeper meanings

Sometimes the deepest meanings of the play that you're writing will not be clear to you until you're well into the process. It may come out of a line of dialogue or a new plot twist, but suddenly the floor of the play opens and you're looking down into a sub-basement of meaning you never knew was there. It's heartening when that happens: your play means more than even you yourself realized!

Characters wiser than you

A student was writing a play with a stupid hero. I suggested the play might be more interesting if the protagonist were smarter. He said, "But I can't write a character who's smarter than I am." In discussing this, I realized that he could. So can you.

---

96 https://en.wikipedia.org/wiki/The_Ecstasy_of_Rita_Joe

For one thing, there's the simple matter of timing: you can give a character a quick comeback which you've laboured over for weeks. But in another, deeper way, your characters can be smarter, wiser, better than you—can understand things you don't understand, or didn't think you understood. As you write them, you come to understand those things too, and become a little smarter, wiser, better, yourself. It is one of the great joys of playwriting: the moment when a character you're writing says something so lovely that you think, "I wish *I'd* thought of that."

Find the joy in the work, and have fun

Talent exists, and most people have it, but it's overrated, except in the case of a very few geniuses who have a ridiculous amount. In my opinion, what separates the artists from everybody else is not so much talent as a deep enjoyment of the actual work.

We all try out different art forms when we're kids. We experiment on musical instruments, we sing, draw, paint, sculpt, write poems, try acting. We dream of being successful, renowned artists. But most us discover that we're not as good at these pursuits as we had hoped, or not improving quickly enough, and we compare our first drafts to the finished masterpieces of great artists, and we give up.

I think successful artists are the ones who love simply *doing* it so much that their enjoyment gets them through that discouraging phase when they're not noticeably good at it yet. Eventually, through sheer, determined practice, they get skillful enough that people start to praise what they think is their talent.

The difference between the beginning artist and the seasoned artist is not that the seasoned artist makes fewer mistakes. It is that the beginning artist says, "Oh, I made that same mistake again. That means I'm no good at this, I don't know what I'm doing and I should quit." The seasoned artist says, "Oh, I made that same mistake again. Let's find some cool new way to fix it."

You need to enjoy the actual activity more than you love the dream of being successful. That means enjoying its component activities. (I take pleasure in typing.) There are always discouraging moments when feeling that joy is not easy. You have to find all the ways you can, big and small, to make it pleasant for yourself.

Have fun. That's not just a friendly farewell at the end of this book; it's also the best advice I can give you about being an artist. If you find out from this book, or from your own efforts, that you *are* a playwright, please gain other experience in the theatre as well. Join a theatre company, student, amateur, or professional. Act, direct, paint sets, or organize props. Sit in on rehearsals. Observe how the director, designers, and actors interpret the script. Keep your own copy, and track the notes and changes. If the playwright is present in rehearsal, observe how and why the script changes are made.

But if you learn that you're *not* a playwright, well, you're in good company. Of the thousands of students I've taught, only a handful have become playwrights, though I hear that what others have learned has been helpful to them elsewhere. If you're one of those others, do find a form of expression that calls to you, and practise it professionally or as an amateur. The arts can be a great, meaningful consolation in this often bumpy and surprising life.

Above all, have fun doing the work itself. This applies to the writing of a deep tragedy as much as a light farce. It's a principle I wish I had discovered earlier in my own career. Lately, my chief concern as I write is the question, "Am I having a good time?" Keep asking yourself that. And if you're not having a good time, stop, take another look at what you're doing, alter it until it's fun again—and keep writing. It is called "*play*-writing," after all.

INDEX

Acknowledgements

I'd like to thank my editor, Glenda MacFarlane of J. Gordon Shillingford Publishing; my consultant, Lin Bennett; Annie Gibson of Playwrights Canada Press, Rebecca Burton of the Playwrights Guild of Canada, Steven Green of the Fulton Theatre, Mitchell Lazarus, Emma Lazarus Heyland, Naomi Lazarus Baker, Joan MacLean, and my writers' group The Inkstons: Ian Coutts, Bruce Geddes, Patricia Henderson, Catherine Lyons-King, Cameron Smith, Morgan Wade, and Corina Zechel. My apologies to anyone whose name I may have inadvertently omitted. I also wish to thank all those individuals and their representatives—whether they are personal friends, colleagues and acquaintances, or strangers to me—who have so kindly permitted me to quote them and/or tell stories about them. Finally, a deep thank you to Kevin Loring, for his Foreword; to Kevin Kerr and Tracey Erin Smith for their comments; to Studio 58 of Vancouver and the Dan School of Drama and Music at Queen's University of Kingston, where I spent so many happy years teaching; and to all the students, friends, family, and fellow artists who have taught me so much over the decades.

John Lazarus

John Lazarus grew up in Montreal, graduated from the National Theatre School's Acting program in 1969, and then worked for 30 years in Vancouver as an actor, advertising copywriter, TV and radio broadcaster, critic, screenwriter, playwright, and teacher. He taught Playwriting and Solo Show Techniques for 10 years at Vancouver's Studio 58, and in 2000 moved to Kingston, where he taught over 2,500 drama students at Queen's University, until retiring in 2021. John's own plays, produced across Canada and around the world, include *Babel Rap, Dreaming and Duelling, Village of Idiots, The Late Blumer, Homework & Curtains, Genuine Fakes, The Nightingale, Medea's Disgust, Rough Magic, Trouble on Dibble Street, The Grandkid*, and his series of plays for children, published under the title *Not So Dumb*. He lives in Kingston with his wife, Lin, and they have children and grandchildren in Toronto and Vancouver.

To learn more about John's work, go to johnlazarus.ca